This Enchanting Place
Facets of Chalice Well

Edited by Ann Procter

published by
Chalice Well Bookshop
Chilkwell Street
Glastonbury
Somerset
BA6 8DD

Tel: (01458) 831154
email sales@chalicewellshop.com
www.chalicewellshop.com

© Chalice Well Trust 2006
www.chalicewell.org.uk
edited by Ann Procter
design and layout by Lloyd Drew
printed by St Andrew Press, Wells

ISBN 0-9552795-0-X
       978-0-9552795-0-8

Contents

Illustrations

Introduction by Ann Procter

There is no doubt that many people find Chalice Well enchanting at a deep level. Something here makes the heart sing (chant). Sufi mystics say that spirituality is the tuning of the heart, and one can obtain it neither by study, nor by piety. It's not only the heart which resonates, it's that special core within the heart which opens to the soul or spirit. Being at Chalice Well often helps to make that connection more real. This has nothing to do with any particular religion, faith or sect, so there are no constraints, oughts or shoulds, just the opportunity to experience something which helps progress along a spiritual path. In 1959, Wellesley Tudor Pole (most often known as WTP), when setting up the Trust, remarked that after his first visit to the Well in 1904 he was "left with the premonition that in time to come I should be given the opportunity of coming into possession of this truly wonderful place, so that it might be thrown open to Pilgrims of every faith and race." So many people feel drawn to the special atmosphere, which motivates them to provide what is necessary to maintain Chalice Well at every level from spiritual to material, indeed for some it is almost an addiction.

This booklet aims to express how the contributors experienced this place. They have all volunteered, or agreed most readily when asked, to present their scripts. No bribery was needed! As editor I have not dictated the content or style, only giving a limit to the number of words, and discussed a minimum of amendments needed. So all the facets are uniquely creative. They are called 'facets' rather than 'chapters', because I see them as different faces glowing on a diamond depending on how the light catches it. To use another analogy: if you visit an art class, all the students are focussed on representing the object displayed before them, but if you walk round observing the various easels, each will be unique, not only in the completed picture seen from different angles, but in the medium used, and in the feelings of the artist being expressed about the object.

Most of the colour illustrations are gifted to our use by Ann Cook, a local professional photographer. The booklet is enveloped in two angels: on the inside front cover the stone statue overlighting a seat in the garden; on the inside back cover a picture painted by a Russian child. She came with a group from Chernobyl to experience the healing peace of Chalice Well, and left us this impression.

There is no need to read the Facets in any particular sequence, just dip into them as the spirit moves, but for convenience I will introduce them in the order in which they appear in the booklet.

In **Facet One** we go back in history to the time of Alice Buckton, who looked after the Well in the first part of the 20th century. Tracy Cutting, who was on the staff at the Well for a time, took a special interest in this remarkable lady, and gives us a cameo portrait. If your appetite is whetted, read Tracy's book called "Beneath the Silent Tor".

In **Facet Two** we hear the view of the Founder, WTP, who built upon the Trust initiated by Alice Buckton. Paul Fletcher is our volunteer archivist at the Well, and has put together some history and revealing quotations.

Next, **Facet Three**, gives memories from the second half of the 20th century. Mrs Phyllis Bourne (known everywhere as "Pip") and her late husband Arthur, gave huge amounts of their time and energy to Chalice Well. When, in her eighties, she retired as a Trustee, we encouraged her to make a tape of her memories, and this is a selection, which I have made with difficulty as I would have liked to include them all. Mary Priest-Cobern, a current Trustee, did the laborious task of transcribing the tape. Pip is now living in East Anglia, near her family, and

6

has recently passed her 95th birthday. She still drinks the healing water, now in homoeopathic form. (Posting small dropper bottles is easier and cheaper than transporting the original water) . There is no doubt that Arthur and Pip lived under the spell of Chalice Well for many years!

Yes, it IS healing water! Caroline Sherwood, in **Facet Four**, has researched the archives and current reports resulting in a large number of healing stories to gladden your heart. Her facet includes a photo of the pool in Arthur's Court when it was much deeper.

The Origin of the Waters has long been an interest of Nicholas Mann, who gives his view in **Facet Five**. Nicholas is a Staff member at the Well, with special responsibility for the Companions' Register, and his many published works are available in the bookshop, and via the website.

I would like to put in a word here about scientific investigations into measuring the healing abilities of Chalice Well water. Douglas Dean, an American professor of physics, alas now dead, worked with water held between the hands of a spiritual healer. He found that water so treated absorbed infra red light at a unique wavelength of 2.7 microns. By measuring the degree of IR light absorption relative to "ordinary tap water". he had a figure for the water's healing ability. He concluded that water showing a ratio of more than 0.035 had some degree of healing properties up to a maximum of 0.080. He then measured some other sources of water with the following results: London tap water 0.024, Lourdes water from taps available to pilgrims 0.026, Findhorn spring water 0.049, Chalice Well water from the Lion's Head 0.059, Lourdes water from the original spring 0.070. We also looked at Chalice Well water by Polycontrast Interference Photography, a computerised form of Kirlian photography, and found significantly more light around the aura of "our" water, especially at the Lions' Head, and from the flow in Wellhouse Lane, when kept in glass rather than plastic containers. This was before the assessment offered by Prof. Graeffe, which showed an even greater enhancement at the bottom of the Flowform.

Maybe it's not just the water in some cases, but the sacred site as a whole which makes fundamental changes in a person, by accessing their souls? John Rowntree, who was a Trustee from 1995 - 97 wrote "The Well gives forth virgin water from the purest source of timeless origin. It is our purpose to facilitate the potential of each individual visitor to benefit personally and uniquely by offering beauty to one or all of their five senses, so that the Creator's lamp lodged within each person may be kindled by the sparkle of the water, and the love of us all".

Which brings us to **Facet Six**, from Head Gardener, Ark Redwood. You will usually find Ark somewhere around: a lanky figure, dressed in green, like some mobile bush transplanted wherever he happens to be working, offering a blossoming smile to all who greet him.

His attention to the nature spirits is also addressed in **Facet Seven**, from Danu Forest, a volunteer helper in the garden, whose special talent for awareness of subtle influences at the Well enlarges our understanding and experience. Her approach illustrates one of the MANY kinds of spiritual paths followed by visitors. Featuring more of them would have required a much larger book ! We have included another one in the colour photographs: there have been Buddhist retreats, in association with which beautiful mandalas were made. A group of monks spent several days meticulously tapping in coloured sands, and then the finished article was dedicated to world peace.

Facet Eight comes from Sig Lonegren, a current Trustee. He is known worldwide for his dowsing and teaching and offers relevant differing, and co-existant, views of the geomantic situation at the Well

Then we come to another person offering her service: Jen Wakefield is a gatehouse volunteer, obviously under the spell, and happy to be so. That's **Facet Nine**.

In **Facet Ten** my husband Roy tells of his involvement as a Trustee over 14 years of big changes at the Well. At the beginning he describes our first visit to the Upper Room, which had a profound effect on us both. I also remember walking up a rough track past Little St Michael's Retreat House - no pergola or paved path – then giving my dues to a lovely lady (probably Pip) sitting in a little wooden hut covered with ivy. She had WTP's books for sale and gave us a brief guide on a board to return after our visit. We walked through a small wooden gate, then up the path to the Well. It was rough, between overgrown bushes and lots of brambles, nothing like the beautiful gardens of today, but the Well itself was magical, and I was hooked!

In **Facet Eleven**, the current staff give us an idea of their busy BUSY activities, keeping the place and all its connections grounded and efficient. The quotes about how they feel about being here show that they surely would not be involved if their hearts were not drawn to it.

Then there are folks who love the place from far away. Sarah Stewart lives in Canada, and has run courses at the Well, her group staying in Little St Michael's. She shares their experiences in **Facet Twelve**.

From America Michael Calabrese gives views from "Across The Pond" from himself and friends in **Facet Thirteen**. Their messages are all about the impact of Chalice Well on the lives of others, and the need to be here again – soon.

At the end there is a short appendix, researched for us by Alison Stenning, in case some of the names and dates need clarification as you read the scripts.

We have added a note of practicalities to encourage you to visit, and our bookshop manager offers a list relevant books for further reading.

Please enjoy! And be at peace in our love from this enchanting place.

Alice Buckton

Facet One

In the Time of Alice Buckton
by Tracy Cutting

It is a cold, crisp autumn morning, and a young girl approaches the school courtyard. To her right stands the imposing gothic-style building, home to students and pilgrims, and called 'The Chalice Well School of Sacred Drama and Pilgrim's Rest'. As the young girl walks across the cold stone a figure appears from the shadows. Dressed in a black cloak and large black hat the figure glides towards the girl. "What are you doing here?" enquires the figure. "Please Miss, I'm here for rehearsals, but I'm a little early" the anxious child responds. "Well don't just stand there, why don't you do something useful? Here, take this broom and sweep the leaves". The child, half in awe and half in fear, begins to sweep the yard until rehearsals are about to begin. "I must not argue with Miss Buckton" she whispers to herself, "I must do my best for her as she does for us". The child was 8 years old and a member of the Glastonbury Community. The lady in black, Alice Buckton, who purchased the Chalice Well in 1913 and had dedicated 30 years of her life to protecting 'her mother centre' and in creating and promoting the art of sacred drama.

Alice had purchased the Chalice Well Site at auction, and the gothic building was all that remained of the junior seminary which was located here until a few years before. Alice had fierce competition at the auction, including a wool merchant who planned to use the spring as a means of powering his machinery! Thankfully, Alice won the day. and began to lay the foundations of what would become a place for pilgrims, students and the sacred.

Alice originally planned to open the school as a traditional facility for young ladies, however, within a short period of time Alice and her companion, Annette, had abandoned these ideals and transformed the area into a creative space for dances, plays and pageants, all being written, designed and performed within the grounds. Her most popular play was 'Eager Heart', a Christmas Mystery, which was performed mainly at the Well, but also in the town (Assembly Rooms and St John's Church) and throughout the country. For each production the resident students and house guests, as well as the local community, would make every item required for the production. From the gardens they used vegetables to make dyes to colour homemade cloth. The woodworking classes and metalworkers would make props, and seamstresses would sew individual feathers onto the angel's wings.

Alice worked by the 'Arts and Crafts Movement' philosophy, and so very little money ever exchanged hands at productions, as content was more important than the cost. To help support the upkeep of the Well students produced beautiful ceramics and enamelled jewellery, which was sold at 'The Corner Bookshop' in Glastonbury High Street. Few guests ever seem to have paid for their keep either, often contributing in practical ways instead, such as the composer, Gustav Holst, who once wrote a piece for a production of Eager Heart, and later adapted it to become part of 'The Planets'.

In addition to her passion for teaching, and for sacred drama, Alice was an accomplished poet with a number of books published, and hundreds of others held safe in her own collection. Her topics ranged from observational 'news' items to the sacred and profound. Fundamentally a Christian, it is through her writings that we see beneath the outer veneer to the complicated and private person beneath. It is here we find her interest in the esoteric, in her belief in the Grail Legends, of her passion for nature, and her quest for spiritual knowledge.

In 1922 Alice united the communities of Glastonbury, Street and Wells when, together with the Town Council, she produced a black and white moving picture, called 'Glastonbury Past and Present'. The film was the first of its kind – a promotional drama to encourage visitors to the historic town and its many interesting features. For a whole year the town and surrounding areas were alive with excitement as costumes were made, scripts written and re-written and rehearsals staged. Four hundred members of the local community took part in the film, all amateurs with the exception of one! Townsfolk were united as their masterpiece was recorded, in less than ideal conditions, and later shown to packed audiences in the local cinemas. It was an outstanding success, but with limited appeal outside of the area, it failed to meet the expectations of those involved, and few other cinemas screened what has become a piece of classical Glastonbury history.

The creative freedom which cinema offered appealed to Alice, and it is known that she had hoped to film a production of Eager Heart, and various of her other works, and to travel around the U.K and the world with them, promoting herself and the work being undertaken at Chalice Well. Sadly, like many of her grand plans, this plan never seems to have reached fruition and 'Glastonbury Past And Present' is the only known recorded work, and an original copy is held by the British Film Institute in London.

Alice Buckton was a unique woman; an educational reformer, a poet, teacher and visionary. She gave everything she owned to protect the Well for future generations so that "all men and women of good heart may visit here". She was determined, focused and an independent spirit. Her associate, Wellesley Tudor Pole, once remarked that she was like a spoilt child, used to stamping her feet and getting her way. But it was that true grit which enabled her to protect this special space for more than 30 years. Her spirit lives on in the many musical and dramatic presentations offered within the grounds of Chalice Well each year, which are open to all to attend, and her wish for a secure future for the Well was finally realised, some years after her death, when Wellesley Tudor Pole purchased the old school house, May Cottage, Vine Cottage, St Michael's and, of course, the grounds including the ancient Well Head. Forming the modern day Trust, which incorporated Alice's original Trust, the Chalice Well was finally safe for future generations to enjoy.

Wellesley Tudor Pole

Facet Two

As Seen By Wellesley Tudor Pole
by Paul Fletcher

*"There is not enough darkness in the whole world to
extinguish the light of a single candle."*

W.T.P. in a letter to Sir David Russell 15-5-1940

WTP first visited the site of the Chalice Well in the spring
of 1904, on his second visit to Glastonbury. In those
days entrance to the well was governed by the Roman
Catholic Seminary, which stood at the lower end of the site
by the road. The only approach for the public was through a
green locked doorway known as the Monk's Entrance at the
lower end of the wall in Wellhouse Lane. There was an old
fashioned handle by this door, which rang a bell in the
quadrangle of the Catholic College. WTP had to wait some
time before a very "ancient dame" from the College kitchen
unbolted the door, and demanded one shilling from him. He
was then directed up through a ruined area, now Arthur's
Courtyard, through a cabbage patch garden, until the well
itself was reached.

This did not look at all promising. The area was forlorn
and unkempt, and visitors were not made welcome, but
often turned away. The wellhead was covered by a wooden
slab without a hinge. WTP drank the waters and roamed over
the garden and orchards, and the slopes of Chalice Hill. Yet
the young Wellesley was so affected by the atmosphere
around the well that he knew in these moments that one day
he would be given the opportunity to restore the site. Not
many would have had the focus and determination to wait
for 55 years for this to come to pass. He later recorded that
the whole place seemed absolutely familiar as though he had
been there all his life.

During those 50-odd years things moved on, of course, both in WTP's life, and at the Chalice Well. There was the involvement with John Goodchild, which led to the discovery of 'the blue bowl' at Beckery, and the subsequent work undertaken with the bowl across Europe, and in Britain. Alice Buckton travelled regularly to Clifton, in Bristol, to visit WTP and she was present at the Dean's Yard meeting on July 20th 1907 in London, when the Archdeacon of Westminster presided over a gathering of about fifty people to examine the blue bowl.

When the First World War started WTP was managing director of a flour, cereal and grain merchants. He enlisted in 1916 and was awarded an O.B.E. in 1919 for "valuable services in connection with military operations in Egypt." This included his part in rescuing Abdul Baha Abbas, son of the founder of the Baha'i Movement in Haifa. He quickly became conscious of the growing threat from Nazi Germany. In 1934 he wrote to David Russell, "Apart from inner training and preparation, I do not know what each of us can do whilst watching the approach of world shaking events. To avoid a sense of impotence in the face of what is coming is by no means easy!" He felt humanity was caught between two huge waves of spiritual power, and that many would drown in the coming conflict. To offset the negative effects he began to introduce the idea of 'The Silent Minute' to members of the Government, a time each evening at 9 o'clock when silent contemplation and prayer would be held by a growing number of people throughout the world. Launched in the spring of 1940 conservative estimates of those involved four years later were around 10 million people.

As regards Glastonbury he had worked ceaselessly from 1903-1931 to link Avalon, Iona and Eiron (Devenish Island, Northern Ireland) and to awaken these sites for the coming era. He had concluded that Glastonbury would not have awakened without Chalice Well being brought back to life and that the restoration of Iona, linked to Glastonbury, was important for the future destiny of Britain. Thus it was, that after over fifty years of waiting, the grounds of Chalice Well became available for purchase and his friends, the first 'companions', were able to support it financially.

So what were WTP's deeper thoughts on Chalice Well at the close of the 1950's? Fortunately for us he wrote soon afterwards to Rosamond Lehmann:

"There are certain geographical spots or centres where, for reasons too complex to explain shortly, the veil is 'thinner' than elsewhere. There may be historical, occult or even astrological reasons that have supervened over the centuries to bring about this thinning of the veils, through which Light can pass down into our human atmosphere more easily than is the case elsewhere.

"Such spots are nearly always associated with a healing Spring or Well, and with holy persons from past history. At such spots, if they are preserved, peacefully and prayerfully, pilgrims can not only find rest, but their inner perceptions can be stimulated and brought out into the open.

"Chalice Well is one such centre, and part of its heritage is to be able to act like a sounding board: i.e., whatever is thought or done there becomes magnified and carries further than is the case with more ordinary spots or sites. With the world in turmoil, the careful preservation of such dedicated centres becomes imperative for the welfare of the 'whole' community."

Personally, WTP's vision was more intensely focused and grander still in its view of the future. He thought of Chalice Well as the first Gateway in Britain through which Christ's message entered, and he felt the task of the Well was to render the property (i.e. the dwellings and the garden laid out in a particular way) and its atmosphere peaceful, beautiful and worthy to be used again as "a Gateway for a message for the Coming Times."

In an earlier piece of writing he had said: "The Druids and the ancient Sun Worshippers knew a thing or two.

Although the Chalice Well Spring in those days was deep in a forest, it was here that they constructed their Tree Temples, and held their Services and Rituals. No doubt that Joseph of Arimathea was sent here by interior gravitation because the atmospheric conditions were most suitable from which to proclaim the Christ message. No doubt the presence at this spot of saintly men and women over many centuries has tended to further sanctify this centre which in its way is unique...the most important evidence will, of course, be forthcoming when the Keynote Message for the New Age is sounded from Chalice Well and radiated across the world from there."

Here we have the distillation of WTP's vision for the Chalice Well adventure. A place of sanctity, used by the ancient ones, by the pagan streams, overlaid with the true messages of Christ and now being cared for at the beginning of the Aquarian Age, at a time of great opening, by a transient community of souls who must strive to embody all these things in a rainbow vision.

That he was able to secure all this land and property is a remarkable achievement. The Tor School was added in 1966 and with the orchards on Chalice Hill and the field on the Tor side of Wellhouse Lane the estate covered about twelve acres. By the mid Nineteen-Sixties Tudor Pole was already suffering from the illness which would end his life in September 1968 but he continued to bring through his vision and anchor it into the material world. High on the agenda was the creation of an 'Upper Room' in Little St. Michaels, dedicated to silence, meditation and prayer. His glimpses, an unusual form of 'seership,' are chronicled in his writings 'A Man Seen Afar,' Writing On The Ground,' and 'The Silent Road,' where we can travel alongside WTP on his cosmic voyaging. WTP's glimpse of the house where the Last Supper was held led him to create this Upper Room sanctuary. It has been called a "supreme act of creative imagination" which allows us a starting point to voyage into the spaces of our interior vision.

The blue bowl remained with WTP at his house in Hurstpierpoint, in Sussex, and he was unsure of where it should reside. He was well aware of the significance of a smooth transition from the Era of the Cross to the Era of the Chalice and felt the symbolism and actuality of this transfer was intended to take place first in Avalon and at Chalice Well, which would eventually lead to a unification of all faiths and peoples. This is grand stuff! He even conjectured the union of the chalice of the west and the lotus of the east. However, the factual and material history of the blue bowl remained veiled and hidden from all his efforts. He wrote in 1966, "it can and should be regarded as the insignia of the New Era now approaching, when the Cup will replace the Cross as the sign manual of the single and Universal Faith destined to lead humanity forward toward the ultimate goal of the Golden Age." But still he wrote of "when and if this vessel is deposited in the Upper Room the Chalice Well trustees as a whole will become responsible for it. However, one thing is certain. Had it not been for the recovery of the cup in 1906 Avalon and Chalice Well would still lie supine in the shadows, impotent to play a major part in the re-awakening of Britain and her people in their potential spiritual destiny."

Here once again are the component parts of Tudor Pole's vision. The establishment of a healing garden around the ancient blood well laid out with care and spiritual intention (see 'My Dear Alexis - letters to Rosamond Lehmann') and a retreat house for pilgrims and visitors which includes the Upper Room, thus creating a matrix for spiritual outpouring to the world. The Silent Minute, The Lamplighter Movement, and The Chalice Well restored and renewed. These were the gifts TP gave us from his life work.

At Companion's Day in 1966 he addressed companions: "This is a place of sanctity where heaven and earth can meet and where the visible can merge naturally into the unseen. The visionary is often derided for what he feels and sees, and yet we are told on high authority that the very life of a people is imperiled when vision has departed from among them. Some of you have shown anxiety because the barque of our adventure has recently sailed through stormy seas and at times has seemed to find it difficult to retain an even keel. Why should we be surprised at this?

"We are engaged on re-kindling a lamp at Chalice Well, a lamp that once burned brightly, but has been allowed over the centuries to flicker and fade away."

He then went on to stress the importance of the work in the gardens with the nature kingdoms: "It has always been our intention that Chalice Well activities should give pride of place to the healing of mind and body through the agency of the Spirit, with the co-operation of Nature. If we are willing to show friendliness and compassion toward those who control the Kingdoms of Nature, they in turn will help us to restore health and well-being to our minds and bodies, and to harmonize the conditions which surround us."

His final message on that day in August 1966 was about Chalice Well's role in the world. He finished, "where better than Chalice Well to sow the seeds of such a purpose and tend them carefully, under the guidance of the 'Revealer of the Word' whose unseen presence is already in our midst?"

In these words we can hear WTP in his last years trying to convey to all of us who would read his work in the coming years a sense of what Chalice Well could mean in the future. He was imparting information from what he called 'au dela,' trying to communicate so that we might grasp something of what this is all about. Even in his eighties TP was still open enough to welcome the 'flower children' to the gardens and also to write in a letter to Rosamond Lehmann about the Beatles, their music and their interest in eastern mysticism. He was well aware that Chalice Well as a 'project' would often be beset by turbulence and adversity – what he called "superficial clashes and discords" – but that these setbacks were of "an illusory kind", and that nothing could affect the fulfilment in due time of the underlying purpose. There would always be fluctuations created by human free will, but gradually and inexorably the unfoldment of a great purpose would be revealed.

This purpose became more sharply focussed as Iona and Devenish continued in their quiet ways, and Glastonbury began to wake up (see Patrick Benham's 'The Avalonians'). The fundamental keynotes at Chalice Well, as proposed by Tudor Pole, are expectation, joy, unity and service. Through the waters of the well, the waters that are also in process of changing their qualities from Pisces to Aquarian rhythms, the keynotes will be expressed.

Let us finish with some words from 'God is Love?' a small leaflet co-produced by The Big Ben Council and the Chalice Well Trust in the 1960's: "The more love we reflect and share with one another, the greater will be the supply available to us: a supply that is infinite, boundless, never failing and eternal. When the truth of this realisation is recognised and utilised we shall be on the first lap of the road leading to the arrival of 'Heaven on Earth'."

Facet Three

Old Time Memories
from a tape by Pip Bourne

In autumn 1966, my "Old Man", Dr Arthur Bourne, after a big operation, was told by his surgeon to go on a holiday before hoping to go back to work. We did not know where to go, we were not hotel people. Then we saw mention of Chalice Well in a book. and he remembered he had been there in 1925! We looked at each other, grinned, and decided to have a go. John Simmons, the Warden, had himself just arrived 10 days previously with his wife Ida . We visited Chalice Well every day, drank the waters there and "Old Man" grew stronger.

Next Spring, John was asking for volunteers to come for a working holiday. By that time, "Old Man" was much fitter and we applied for a week after Easter. On arrival, John told us he nearly contacted us to tell us not to come as the workman had just finished the central heating two days previously, and the only two clean rooms were the kitchen and our bedroom. When we got to the end of the week we were tired, yes, but very happy! We had also gained two very good friends. After that we came down regularly – about twice a year. Sometimes for John and Ida to have a small holiday, and sometimes to spend our time with them.

We never met WTP, the Trust's Founder. He used to ring us up each time we stood in at Chalice Well. A real sense of humour came over the wires to us. I still have a letter from him where he wanted us to know that the royal family knew about Chalice Well and a member would visit us one day. (And Prince Charles did!)

WTP's vision of the Upper Room became manifest in the loft of Little St Michael's, and it was consecrated in 1967. The date is in the bottom left of one of the windows. You can read about the origin of this vision in his books.

During the years the net curtains dividing the two halves of the room, so carefully chosen by WTP, became grubby and John was worried about washing them. While they were away on their next holiday, I gathered my courage in - I unhooked, washed - ever-so-carefully, and then re-hooked. So sweet and fresh once more. The Blue Bowl was kept in the Room. The satin kerchief wrapped around it was made by Kitty, WTP's sister. It was torn and dirty. John asked me if I would repair it, or try to. Again, I gathered my courage in, mended, embroidered, washed and returned. Again John grinned and was pleased! I loved the sheen on the carved wooden casket containing the bowl and would polish it very lovingly.

The gardens were new when I first met them. Not many plants and not many bushes. Jude looked after the garden in those days, and when complemented on his really lovely roses, we would say every time, "it's that manure that does it". One day he told me he was going to plant a lot of seeds. "Now" says I, "oh no" says he..."not in her right time - but please don't say that to anybody – they will say I was queer". Opinions certainly have changed in the last forty years! We now sell books on that subject in the Bookshop. Later on Gladys and I did quite a bit of gardening at Chalice Well. We would be weeding away – then suddenly she or I would stop and say "look up - and enjoy it all"! And we did! I was told that the big tree at the top, on the left of the garden, was where WTP sat receiving inspiration for his books. I sat there when we had the candlelight vigil one spring, it was indeed good! One day, I was sitting on my haunches; I had stopped weeding, and told Taras I was listening to the birds singing. Listen carefully he said, their song is different in the morning when they are working, than their song in the afternoon, when they are playing.

One day sitting in the corridor seat upstairs I was patching and mending the linen with a lovely companion. She is Dutch, translated TP's books into the Dutch language,

24

and lived in a small castle on an island in Holland, a Dutch Countess. I thought I was not too bad with my needle, but her lovely long fingers flew over her work. We were laughing, she was telling me anecdotes of her life, when the then housekeeper came and reminded us that there was a Trustee meeting in progress downstairs – please would we make less noise! Afterwards we giggled, like two guilty schoolgirls.

There was Snook the cat, a lovely, lively black kitten. Oh, I can see him now, racing, leaping, over and around the beds and bushes to the kitchen door at the sound of a spoon – food! Unfortunately he went wild and disappeared. But one day much later, I bent to pick up a piece of paper from under a bush, when I was walking up the garden, and an infuriated black cat attached itself to my arm and hand with teeth and claws. I kept still and slowly jaws relaxed, claws retracted – it was Snook. He recognised me and rolled on his back, and did all he could to say how sorry he was to have attacked me. We talked together a while, and suddenly he was gone. I never saw Snook again. I went and washed my arm and hand in the waters. They were bleeding rather freely by then. The next day all was healed.

One day I was sitting in the Gatehouse. when a little old lady came in, and gave me an envelope. Please would I keep it for 5 minutes before opening it? She smiled sweetly at me and left. In 5 minutes time, I opened the envelope - £100 with a note "I was healed by the waters here long ago and have saved this for Chalice Well".

However hard we tried, we seemed to be existing on not even a shoestring, but half a shoestring, and we could not pay off any of the overdraft. Then, that precious day, that special Trustee Meeting, when Charles, the then Chairman, told us that a very dear friend of Chalice Well had given us a substantial amount of money. Our overdraft could be paid off, and we would have money to work with. There was perfect silence. No one moved. No one spoke. Then suddenly Taras leapt up and did a war dance of joy. I cannot remember much of the rest of the meeting. We all felt euphoric.

The gardens had to be closed for a while at one time. Then, with the consent of the Chairman, we decided to try and tidy up for re-opening the following Easter. A local lass suggested advertising for labour, and five people volunteered. We seven worked hard those winter months. We opened to an early Easter with an article in the local paper – two photographs – "Old man" with his broom brushing the channels, and me with a robin on my trowel. That robin became very tame and would come to the Gatehouse for, oh not biscuits, but cheese! The visiting children loved to watch him. There was a long queue waiting to come in at 10 o'clock. We were tired but very content at the end of that day. Two of those volunteers were Moya and Taras, who became our next Custodians.

When the cottage was decorated for them, we discovered, much to our horror, that the structure was unsound. Our Guardian Angels were definitely looking after us at that time! The large beams had been within a half an inch of collapsing. As the ceiling came down, so did the straw filling that was used in olden days. The repairs were slow, the builder was ill, the money was tight, but very slowly it began to take shape. One day "Old Man" suggested they move in although work was not yet finished. Moya in her quiet way said "we will as soon as you make us the bed like the one you have made for yourselves" … "Old man" came home, ordered the wood and the work began. When finished, he delivered it and good to her word Moya moved into Vine. Sean was born a few days later. That Christmas Day the four of us went to the Lion's Head where Sean was wet fasted, and we all drank the waters.

The first few years of Companion's Day was held in the large hall of the school during the summer holidays. Teas were provided on a long school room table. I was looking forward to my first Companion's Day, as WTP was coming to talk. Unfortunately he was taken ill just before, and someone else read his message. Afterwards the numbers attending dwindled so rapidly, that Companion's Day was discontinued. Then, the first year that Moya and Taras became Custodians, so many people were writing in; please could Companion's Day come back? So that summer we held one. The weather was fine. We put little tables outside the kitchen for lunch and tea. Hot soup was served at the kitchen door, and "help yourself" tables laid with basic foods, all very well accepted by ninety plus happy Companions! Kitty Tudor Pole was there, recognised me, called me over and we had a lovely chat. We had a tiny marquee, and Sir George Trevelyan and Geoffrey Ashe both gave talks. The weather looked fine, but we were worried. It had been raining heavily previously. Then Sir George said, come on, Glastonbury has some powerful saints. Let us all pray to them for a dry day! We did, and it was dry in Glaston, but was raining all way round. Then at 6pm Companion's Day was over and the heavens opened!

Articles sold to raise funds included Silent Minute Lamps. "Old Man" had become intrigued how to cut glass bottles by a mixture of scoring, heat and rhythmic gentle tapping. He found success with cider bottles and made various ashtrays and candle holders with the bottoms and tops. Seeing the middle of the bottle unused, I lovingly said, "why not a lamp?" He made one, with wooden base, wire and plug all complete. Taras put it on show and it was sold the same day. "Old Man" made a great many after that. We used to ask people for empty cider bottles to continue the manufacture.

I remember one particular regular visitor, a small elderly visitor who told me she loved sitting quietly and watching the "little people" going about their work with nature; tending their own special plants. One day she came down laughing, she had seen an old elf in a tree. A very old personage indeed she said.

We were down there part of the time when the old school was demolished; the building was rapidly becoming unsafe. We had no money and it needed rebuilding, and repairs, so sadly it had to come down. Once or twice I watched from Vine (Cottage) window a great heavy ball being hurled against the walls. Then suddenly the resulting devastation. I was fascinated but horrified too; the immense power wielded in that ball – all to be brought to rubble. Then, one evening the ball came down a fraction too near to Anchor Lodge, adjoining the school. and caused damage. Oh dear, calamity, consternation in the town! Anchor Lodge, a listed building, by some believed to be the site of an old original Anchor Inn, when the sea waters lapped round the Tor and Chalice Hill, and the spices came from the Far East and were brought up the quays in Cinnamon Lane.

"Old Man" and I loved coming down to Chalice Well - always looking forward to our next visit. One spring time we decided not to go, but to trickle along the southeast coast instead. While enjoying our early morning cup of tea on the fourth morning of our holiday, "Old Man" suddenly looked at me and said, come on, let's go there. I agreed immediately, I knew what he meant.

The healing pool when it was full depth

Facet Four

Healings at Chalice Well
by Caroline Sherwood

Iron Age shards, Roman pottery, and the stumps of yew trees[i] indicate that "this great spring was doubtless an attractive focus of visitation..."[ii] from very ancient times.

William of Malmesbury[iii] is the first to record the Well; apparently he reported that the water flowed sometimes red and sometimes blue![iv]

In the 18th century, Glastonbury flourished as a spa. In 1751, Matthew Chancellor, from North Wootton (who had been asthmatic for thirty years) had a dream, indicating that he should drink Glastonbury water for seven Sunday mornings in succession. He obeyed the dream - and was cured. This precipitated a massive influx into the town. People were cured of ulcers, 'most difficult and troublesome respiration', wens[v], deafness, rheumatism, a 'cancerous humour of the tongue', King's Evil [vi](or scrofula), paralysis and even leprosy. Ten thousand people were recorded as visiting in one day, and water was bottled and sent to London.[vii]

"*The Virtues and Efficacy of the Waters of Glastonbury*" records colourful and dramatic healing accounts, and the writer assures us "the Things recounted were not done in a Corner, in the Dark, but in the Face of Day, and to the Knowledge of many."[viii]

The qualities of the water itself have been the subject of much discussion. In 1962, the director of Champneys Nature Cure Resort wrote to Wellesley Tudor Pole (after he had sent water samples to him for research) that, if plans for fluoridation became operative, "it would seem that a source such as the Chalice Well will be the only way of obtaining pure water suitable for therapeutic purposes."[ix]

31

Tests in 1967 revealed traces of fine silica, iron and copper – and also slight radio-activity.[x] The most recent analysis (September 2005) showed a high amount of iron and manganese.[xi] The water has been used in making a variety of remedies, and research is being carried out to establish its use in homoeopathy.[xii]

Lynne Orchard is sure the *coldness* of the water was a significant factor in healing her hand from the results of repetitive strain. This is echoed by an American Companion, who wrote, "The water was very cold but my foot and knees and lower back were on fire! I got out... and noticed that my arthritis was gone. P.S. My undies are still stained terra-cotta!"[xiii] Two walkers, who bathed their blistered feet in the healing pool,[xiv] awoke next day with a complete 'sole healing'.[xv]

Wellesley Tudor Pole was convinced that when the water first emerged from the ground its healing properties were 'fixed' and only became available once it had been exposed to light and air. He wrote, "It should be remembered that water can be the carrier or channel for healing energy, but is not the energy itself."[xvi]

Healing at the Well means many things to people and this World Peace Garden is a focus for healing prayers. As well as the traditional rags tied to trees, notes have been found tucked into crevices, and rings, jewellery, crystals and statuettes have been found in the well itself. Most intriguingly, a Doc Marten boot was found tied to a tree in the meadow![xvii]

In 1967 Anne Hill reported the healing of a 'metal allergy'. "Six months previously (my hands) had to be bandaged and I was unable to put them in water, or do the usual work of house and garden."[xviii] Willa Sleath remembers a woman with acute psoriasis who held her hands under the Lion's Head, then plunged them into the rill at Arthur's Court. An hour later the psoriasis had completely gone.

When Alan Angel was 21 he contracted acute industrial dermatitis. Covered with painful psoriatic lesions, he was hospitalised for a few months. The treatment of daily baths, UV light and ointments worked for a while, and then seemed to stop. After bathing at Arthur's Court he was discharged from hospital. "And so my love affair with the spirits of the well and the place began."[xix]

Sally Randall's daughter, Lucy, had severe impetigo[xx]. They visited Chalice Well, and bathed the little girl's legs in the water. On return to school the teacher "could not believe the improvement...She had gone from not being able to bend her legs, to walking into school 24 hours later, without any obvious trace, but the scabs."

A whole book could be devoted to the miraculous healings reported by Gangesh Kumari Kak. She now takes the water to India where she adds it to her well; gives it to her cows and distributes it to all who need it. Her remarkable story began when she was healed of acute cystitis. She entered the gardens "in agony" and drank, and drank, and drank the water. When she left she was symptom free.

Matthew Gough says "...the impact on mental well being is significant...I have on many occasions been able to gain strength from being in the garden, which has enabled reflection and a review of strategies to deal with many issues."

People have reported a whole range of non-physical healings, from healing fear while in the gardens at night,[xxi] to clearing the residual effects of centuries of the energies of warfare,[xxii] to help with recovery from shock and grief.[xxiii]

Sitting on the Angel seat, Val Watson describes a profound reconciliation with her daughter, with whom her relationship had not been an easy one, to say the least. A huge, but subtle, energy of emotion came over both of us, and we cried together, and held each other."

Even addictions, notoriously difficult to heal, are not excluded. An entry in the Gatehouse daybook in September

2005 reads, "For many years I had a love/hate relationship with alcohol (red wine in particular). Two years ago I came to Chalice Well with the intention of severing the connection... Alcohol free for 2 years. I have returned today to cut the ties that bind me to the tobacco God."

During a healing weekend Chris Waters invited her group to step forward and look into the Well, to see if the face looking back had a message for them: "There was a young man in the group (who)... had struggled with depression ...As he looked at the face looking back at him he saw that it was his own face, and yet there was an enigmatic smile at the corners of his mouth...He saw that the face looked contented... He was surprised ... because he could see a new face emerging ... one that he didn't recognise." Within two months he had a girlfriend, and a whole new life was opening up for him.

Some accounts are more esoteric. On a visit in 1992 Jodine Cognato Turner[xxiv] found herself doing 'automatic writing'... "I had a recollection of many women being slaughtered at the Well...it affected me for months afterwards, with...periods of intense longing for something un-nameable, something of the Divine Feminine."

People often report feminine presences, angelic presences, and the presence of a 'White Lady'. Catherine Shaw has come to "completely trust" that every time she visits the Well she feels "a whooshing sound/sensation and sometimes a clear image...of a female white figure." She immediately feels "deep peace, love, acceptance, as if I have been washed inside and out."

When David Lawrey sat at the well head, he noticed that he was forming an equilateral triangle with two 'human' ladies, whilst being aware of "a presence on my inner screen that felt like a lady dressed in white....I felt a rush of energy which appeared to come through my crown...making my whole body vibrate...I was told this was a 'third strand DNA activation'...It was only when I did some internet research that I discovered the theory that many of us are having our 'spiritual' DNA reactivated at this time, in order to help usher in the golden age in the lead up to 2012."

However, being of an esoteric disposition is certainly not a prerequisite for receiving healing. Angela Savage says, "I had no expectation other than it was a peaceful garden. It was like walking into a 'bubble' where time had slowed down and peace descended." While sitting by the spring in the meadow she "felt a powerful presence come close to me, and I was immersed in a feeling of pure unconditional love – I cried and cried. This was so unlike me..."

A young pregnant woman, whom Willa Sleath described as 'ordinary, vibrant, and quite unpretentious' came to the Well. She had cancer, and was wondering whether she should have an abortion. Willa felt very strongly that she shouldn't and, after nine months of drinking the water, she gave birth to a healthy baby, after which she had a course of chemotherapy. When the cancer recurred four years later, she resumed her Well visits; taking huge containers of water home with her. She recovered. Willa commented it was her 'naïveté' which made her healing all the more remarkable.

"I was not into anything regarding religion...I was a bit of a party animal - loads of beer and boyfriends," wrote Beverley Dodds. More recently, after the death of her baby, she came with her partner to the Well to scatter the ashes: "On the day we arrived ...the weirdest thing happened ...We went up to the meadow...but we still couldn't get the box to open and I fell over down the slope. We both fell about laughing, it was as if the place was reminding us...even though it was an important thing we were doing it was also a great day to celebrate life."

It is not just people who receive healing. The day that Biko, her beloved Labrador was put down, Jenny Stephenson visited the Well on her way home from the vet. "As I sat there grief-filled and tearful, in the little sanctuary area near the well, I was inexplicably filled with a great sense of joy and celebration, emanating not from me but from elsewhere." When she left the garden she was singing.

A note in the Day Book in October 2005 reports a visit by a Companion who visits the Chalice Well to collect bottles full of the water for her "ancient cat" who will drink nothing else!

"It's a miracle!" the vet declared when Gangesh's[xxv] paralysed dog walked again, and his terminal prostate condition was completely cured after being bathed with Chalice Well water.

"Even if the water were to dry up. the healing atmosphere would prevail", Dr Martin Israel said in his address to the Companions in 1969

So what is the healing secret of Chalice Well ? The water's purity, beneficial mineral content, and capacity to conduct healing intention? The benediction of centuries of saints and sages? The faith of generations of pilgrims? The inspirational guidance of angelic and devic presences?

Perhaps all these contribute to its power - and something more besides which (happily and magically) will always be beyond definition.

References

[i] Nick Mann, The Cauldron and the Grail, Annenterprise. Glastonbury, 1985

[ii] Philip Rahtz, Glastonbury, Batsford/English Heritage, 1993

[iii] 1095-1143 A Wiltshire-born Benedictine monk, scholar and historian.

[iv] A Guide to Glastonbury, by the Glastonbury Advertising Association. In Tibetan yoga, the central subtle channel is considered to be blue (flanked by the red and white on left and right)!

[v] A cyst formed by obstruction of a sebaceous gland.

[vi] A form of tuberculosis, characterised by swollen lymph glands in the neck. For centuries English and French monarchs were thought to possess the ability to cure it by the touch of their fingers. This became known as "touching for the king's evil."

[vii] This continues in a new form today. People fill their own or souvenir bottles, and phials of Chalice Well water are available as decorative neck pendants from the shop.

[viii] Transcript of manuscript in Archives.

[ix] Letter in the Archives.

[x] Chalice Well Spring Water: An enquiry into its health giving effects. The Messenger. 2. 1967.

[xi]Report of Mendip District Council's Environmental Health Department.

[xii] From Gatehouse day book.

[xiii] Lady Llunna.

[xiv] Complete immersion was once possible in a deeper pool at Arthur's Court.

[xv] David Eastoe.

[xvi] Chalice Well Spring Water. The Messenger. No 2. 1967. Confirmed by the exquisite work of Masaru Emoto.

[xvii] Information supplied by Chris Marshall.

[xviii] The Messenger, No. 7, 1968

[xix] All accounts are extracts from Companions' emails or telephone conversations.

[xx]A contagious bacterial skin infection which forms pustules and yellow crusty sores.

[xxi] Carol Renwick

[xxii] Mo Layton.

[xxiii] Susan Sneddon.

[xxiv] Author of several books set in Chalice Well (published in USA by Xlibris)

[xxv] See above

Facet Five
The Origin of the White Spring and the Chalice Well, Glastonbury: Local or from far away?
by Nicholas R Mann

The White Spring water contains calcium, fluctuates according to rainfall, and emerges from the ground under little or no pressure. Close by, the Chalice Well, or Red Spring water is rich in iron, fairly constant and makes its way upward with such force that its head is currently elevated over three metres. The pressure is so great that the head probably could be raised much higher. Although rising so close together, far above the surrounding water table with only the Tor and Chalice Hill above them, the two springs possess an entirely different nature and this makes accounting for their origin a considerable challenge.

A juvenile origin could account for the origin of the two springs. Juvenile water rises from deep within the ground, where it is superheated, and driven upwards. Such water is usually full of minerals, like the Red and the White Springs; but unlike them, it is usually hot. As the temperature of the water in the springs (11 degrees C., 52 degrees F.,) is consistent with the springs of the area, a juvenile origin for the water is unlikely as water coming from closer to the earth's core nearly always exhibits an increase in temperature.

An artesian origin also could account for the different qualities of the springs. It explains their high position below a small rainfall catchment area. An artesian spring derives its water from higher ground that is a distance away, and not immediately above the spring. The water falls on the high ground as rain and is carried underground, sometimes for considerable distances, until the geological strata allow it to rise to the surface. While an artesian origin cannot be ruled out for the springs, and has been the most popular explanation in the past, the nature of the underlying strata does not support it. Hydrologists agree that the geological strata between the Tor and the surrounding higher ground, such as the Mendips, are unsuitable for carrying water from one place to the other. The area is underlain by heavy clay – known as the Keuper Marl – which is a very poor carrier of water and, in fact, effectively prevents any water rising from below. The water of the Mendip Hills, moreover, is entirely accounted for. Hydrologists can measure the rate of water rising at all the springs at its foot, such as those at Wells, Wookey Hole and even those in the Bristol Channel, and it is equivalent to the rainfall percolating into the hills.

If the water from the two springs is of a more localised and not a deep, distant origin, then any theory of local origin must explain why the Red Spring rises under pressure, why it is so constant and how its mineral content differs from that of the White Spring when the rainfall catchment area for both springs - Glastonbury Tor – is so small. Above all, it must account for the mineral content of the Chalice Well when there is no iron in the area.

After consultation with the local water authority, local hydrologists and geologists, the author put together the following theory. A long time ago, what was to become the Glastonbury part of the world was an ocean floor receiving vast amounts of sediment. Over millions of years, thick and contrasting layers of sediment accumulated. On the bottom were the Lias beds laid down in the Jurassic age (208-146 million years ago). These included the Keuper Marl and the local limestone known as Blue Lias. Above these beds was deposited a layer of softer yellow stone, known as Midford Sandstone. It is this sandstone that forms the Tor. Above that were yet more layers, several hundred metres thick, and at least one of these layers contained huge quantities of iron.

As land masses shifted over the next hundred million years, all these layers lifted upwards to form a plateau. Heavy tropical rains falling on this plateau drained into the soft underlying stone, and water flowing downwards from the surface of the plateau, carried the minerals from the upper layers into the lower. At this time, what is now Britain was crossing the equatorial zone. Over many millions of years, the iron in the upper layers leached into the water and was carried down to be deposited in the layers of sand and shale below. As the iron rich water passed into the lower Midford layers it hardened the sandstone. In some places this hardening effect was more acute than others. It affected large areas, in which iron-rich nodules would form. These nodules, known locally as 'Tor Burrs,' range in size from less than a centimeter to the metre long 'eggstone' on display behind the Abbot's kitchen in the Abbey grounds.

This is a well known process. The erosion of "iron-bearing shales, which stood at that time at a higher elevation than the surrounding limestone," said Professor O. T. Jones in an address to the British Association, "led to the release of the pyrites, which on oxidation gave rise to acidic iron-bearing waters. It was probably due to the activity of such waters passing over the limestone... that the ore in the limestone was formed. Similar waters... would furnish the necessary iron content to those sediments."[1]

Over time, erosion removed all the top layers, and began on the lower Midford Sandstone. But where the iron rich water from the earlier epochs had infiltrated and hardened the sandstone, it resisted erosion, and so began to appear the familiar landscape of the present day. Glastonbury Tor emerged as the iron-impregnated and hardened sandstone that forms its core resisted erosion while the softer stone around it wore away. Within the Tor, however, remains an aquifer – a subterranean water-bearing system – that was created in much earlier times when greater amounts of water filtered through from above. The bottom part of the aquifer, in the heavier and impervious shales and limestones, is heavily saturated with iron. Rain falling on the

Tor is sufficient to keep the aquifer saturated, and because of its size and the impervious clay layers below, the aquifer does not dry up.

When it rains on the Tor, some water is discharged by surface springs, but much of the water finds its way into the aquifer. The top layers of the aquifer quickly fill up and discharge their water – within a week or so – into the White Spring. During dryer times the water is discharged at a much slower rate of flow. The water picks up the calcium present in the limestone layers and deposits these at the White Spring. The water that lies in the lower layers of the aquifer however, has a quite different character. It passes through the denser sediment of the lower layers at a much slower rate and the calcium is filtered out. It picks up the iron of the lower layers, and eventually emerges under the fairly constant pressure, temperature and volume of the Chalice Well.

The Red Spring although fed by the same aquifer, does not fluctuate like the White Spring as its rate of flow is determined by the relatively stable volume and pressure of water in the aquifer as a whole. As the aquifer reaches maximum saturation in the winter months the volume of water does increase slightly however, and in the summer months it decreases. The maximum flow of the Chalice Well in winter is around 25,000 gallons a day, while in summer it falls to around 19,000 gallons a day. This is consistent with local rainfall patterns. The temperature is consistent with the local ground temperature.

Taking the average rainfall for Glastonbury to be twenty-six inches per year and assuming the catchment area of the Red and White Springs to be the Tor, or about one sixth of a square mile, then following the standard equation that allows for one half loss by evaporation and run off, the maximum volume of water to be expected emerging from the area covered by the Tor is in the region of 125,000 gallons a day. This amount agrees with the average daily volume of the Chalice Well, 20,000 gpd, plus the average daily volume of the White Spring, 10,000 gpd, plus the other springs in the area, 90-100,000 gpd. The catchment area formed by the Tor above the Red and White Springs is therefore sufficient to supply their waters.

This theory accounts for the origin, the character, the mineral nature, and the mineral differences between the two springs. If it is true, the waters of the springs are, in effect, 'home brewed.' They do not originate from far away. The waters originate from an aquifer created in highly unusual circumstances below the Tor; and, in fact, water was responsible for creating the Tor, and gave it the shape it has today.

This article is extracted from *Energy Secrets of Glastonbury Tor*, by Nicholas R Mann (Green Magic, 2004)

[1] *Presidential Address to Section C*, British Association, 1930. Quoted from F. Welch and R. Crookall, 1935.

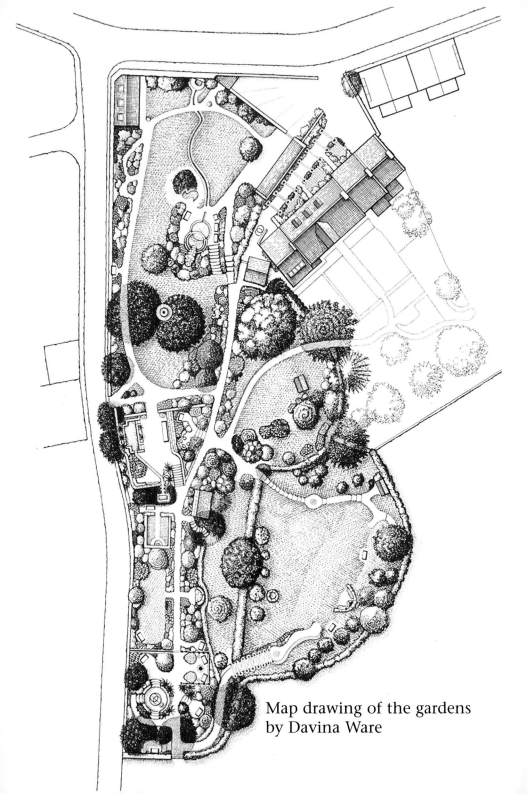

Map drawing of the gardens
by Davina Ware

Facet Six

Cultivating A Sacred Place
by Ark Redwood

Being a gardener at Chalice Well is always a privilege and an honour, and a job of which to be proud. For anyone associated with this place it is patently obvious that this is no ordinary garden. For some people it is a place of pilgrimage, the final destination of an annual quest; somewhere to refresh and renew oneself, as a staging post in the journey of Life. For others, especially the local Glastonbury community, it is the town's 'back garden', a place to bring one's children for a picnic, or to enjoy the swing seats, meet up with friends, or bring visiting relations, as part of the circle of sites, and places of heritage, which abound around the town. Some, of course, simply use this space as a way to experience, and celebrate, the annual cycle of the year, following the dance of the earth, the moon and the sun.

It has to be remembered that Chalice Well is first and foremost a space for spiritual reflection, contemplation, and meditation, and anybody who works within the Garden has to be aware of this fact. Indeed, there can be few gardens in the country where meditators get right of way! Consequently, this inner individual focus has to be borne in mind with regards to the overall design and placing of plants. Whereas it is a common practice in public gardens around the country to go for contrast between plants, particularly with regard to leaf shape and flower colour, here at the Well harmony is the key, and a blending of colour, shape and form is the norm. This means that the inner focus is maintained, and not 'jarred' by a sudden clash of discordance. The 'Chakra Borders' are a case in point, where the colours progress through the spectrum, gradually leading the visitor towards the white section, which merges all the colours into one. On reaching the area around the Well it self, the colours are fairly muted, again, assisting the meditative process.

There can be no doubt that the 'energies' here at the Well possess a special quality. Despite the proximity of the traffic noise, there is an almost tangible stillness here. As many thousands of pilgrims have tasted the waters over the centuries, for healing, or spiritual succour, it's surely not surprising that an 'energy' builds up over time (as has happened with the atmosphere of the Upper Room, in Little St Michael's), and therefore, it can only increase in power in the future.

We gardeners have a duty to ensure that our visitors' experiences are enhanced by the planting, always bearing in mind that some people have travelled halfway across the globe to come here, often for the first time. We want their efforts to be rewarded, by providing a place which thrills their hearts and senses, and leaves them wanting to return again some day.

The style of horticulture which seems to do this best, and the one which prevails here, is traditional cottage gardening, with all the biodiversity that comes with it. This is a tried and tested formula that most people find delightful, with all its variety of plants, buzz of bees, flutter of butterflies' wings and familiar scents, reminiscent of our grandparents' gardens of yesteryear. There is nothing better for encouraging wildlife, and, of course, what one gets as a bonus is a natural, biological way to deal with any pests or diseases. In such a diverse environment the likes of slugs & snails are seen as just a part of the complex web of Life, and welcome to their place within the scheme of things.

Although all of the plants are deliberately chosen and placed, the effect is intended to look naturalistic: not quite 'wild'; and not quite cultivated; but something in between. Usual practice is to position taller plants at the back, and shorter to the front, and to a certain extent this rule is followed, although often it's not. Sometimes, a plant will 'tell' me where it wants to be planted, irrespective of horticultural orthodoxy! Although this apparent randomness can seem 'untidy' to a seasoned garden visitor, most people find it easy on the eye, and one benefit is that there are often plants one missed on one's previous visit. There are many hardy perennials, and self-sown annuals, waiting to burst forth as the spring burgeons out of the apparent bare soils of winter, heralded firstly by the spears of early bulbs, like the snowdrops, crocuses, daffodils and dwarf irises. It is an annual joy to watch this process gather pace each year, culminating in the opulent abundance of May and June, which never fail to delight the senses. Many plants have been selected for their long- or late-flowering season, which extend the colour often into late-October and early November. At this time of year the rays of the westering sun add their own magic touch to the scene. The winter can be a very special time to visit, as the energy moves rootwards, and stillness descends. As visitor numbers naturally reduce, one can often have the Garden to oneself. Those who have experienced this often say that winter is their favourite time to visit, 'but don't tell everyone!'. After the winter solstice, energy begins to stir underground, and come mid-January the first glimmers of green begin to be seen, and the circle turns once more.

Needless to say, we are totally organic (and have been since 2000). Also, all of our composts are peat free, and we try to recycle as much of our resources as we can, (even the Head Gardener's clothes are turned into compost!). The tree leaves are collected and left to rot down for up to two years, and then used to mulch the more woodland-like areas, especially around the Wellhead. All of the woody material is shredded and used to maintain some of the pathways, and naturally the green trimmings, and any other organic material, is added to our compost heaps, which are regularly turned. When well-rotted this is mulched onto the rest of the

Garden. Mulching is preferred to digging, because the latter can be detrimental to the structural stability of the soil. This soil is a living, complex organism comprising a multi-level community of individual creatures and minerals, all weaving their way in, and through, each other. To disrupt this process by digging (i.e. inverting the soil), is best avoided. Circumstances when it is acceptable would be in cases of badly compacted ground, or when it is particularly stony, and structure is poor.

There is a lot more going on in a garden than that which appears to the five senses. There are subtle, yet profound, energies at work co-creating the substance we see all around us. This is the realm of the devas and nature spirits, the faeries and elementals who bring form into being. To the more clairvoyant, and clairsentient, of visitors their presence is clear and obvious. Sometimes all it takes is a quiet time sitting in a corner of the Garden to be alert to their presence, a sense of hushness suddenly surrounds one, and the veils are lifted, and magic takes root.

So, who are these beings of myth and folklore, and what purpose do they fulfill in the greater scheme of things? Well, first of all, I must stress that I'm only stating my opinion, and current understanding of this subject; I could be wrong! How I see it is that the devas hold the etheric blueprint for all forms of life, and the nature spirits bring that form into being. A bit like an architect holding the idea of the perfect building, manifesting a plan, and instructing the workmen how to bring it to fruition.When a seed is sown: for instance, a poppy; what happens is that a blueprint of a 'perfect poppy' is superimposed above and around it, and the nature spirits, (i.e. the intelligent forces of Nature), come into play, and seek to 'inform' its materialization, by utilising the physical environment to bring the etheric 'idea' into physical reality. Therefore, it is beholden on the gardener to always ensure that plants are provided with as optimum conditions as possible, in order for this to happen.

It would be hard work for the nature spirits to expect to nurture a moisture-loving plant if the soil is continually bone dry. They can only work with the environment with which they're provided, so the wise gardener should always bear this in mind. A plant which is thriving will inevitably give off a' happier' vibration than one which is struggling. The key to a partnership between the gardener and the devic realm is simply a matter of learning to be sensitive to these vibrations, and acting appropriately.

Even if one does not accept the existence of these beings, one can surely not fail to feel a certain 'something' in the air, and ground around, which is markedly different from the surrounding land. A bit like stepping into a bubble! For those of us fortunate to work here, we feel truly blessed, and very keen to share this blessing with others. Naturally, and historically, the principle focus has been the Well itself, and quite rightly so. People often travel many miles to be here, to sit at the Well, seeing themselves as pilgrims answering an inner calling, who perhaps feel that being here will provide them with an insight into the next stage of their quest. Experiences people have in the Garden can be very powerful: something simple, like a sudden scent on the breeze; a beautiful dragonfly darting past; the sound of falling water; the recognition of the mandala-like shape of an inflorescence; or the mellifluous trilling of a friendly robin. The Garden provides the backdrop to all these experiences, and much more.

Facet Seven
Goddesses, Devas and Faeries at Chalice Well
By Danu Forest.

The first thing that comes to mind about the Chalice Well is how it has always been a place of sacred pilgrimage to me, as it is for so many others. Living in Glastonbury, my pilgrimage now consists of walking along Chilkwell Street, and with every step I feel I am returning to the 'source'. The Well is a place where my soul is renewed, where I can find stillness amidst the water. Life goes on, with its inevitable ups and downs, but the Well is consistent. Its gurgling stillness gently hushes me, like all those who come to sit by its side. Sometimes gazing into its depths, I am greeted by my own reflection and sometimes by other, stranger visions. The water never ceases its flow, the sunlight and moonlight flicker and dance upon it by turns, as it gushes along its course through the garden. I see friends and strangers come together, and we smile at each other as we drink and are refreshed. It is much more than water that is drunk here, it is spirit.

Sitting by the Well I think back across the thousands of years that people must have come here. How central water is to each of our lives still, and what a gift it is from mother earth, endlessly given. I think of the deep dark places beneath the earth where the water has lain for thousands of years. Like this garden, it must be a still and safe, enclosing place in its ceaseless flow within the hills. I think there is a place inside of me, and all of us, that is like that, a place where my soul dwells. Like the water rising to the surface I want my soul to rise and refresh my life, nourishing me, imbuing my life on the surface with wonder. I believe long ago people who worshipped the Mother saw this place as sacred, long before the Christians came for the same reasons.

I like to think in my own way I continue their line. The word 'Chalice' refers to the grail stories, and to me the grail is another way of seeing the cauldron, a symbol of the Goddess. Whether grail or cauldron, to me it signifies the dwelling place of the soul, and the source of creation. The Red Spring which feeds Chalice Well is the Goddess' cauldron to me, the womb of the earth.. The red of its iron rich water is to me the sacred blood of the Goddess, reflected in every woman's body, balanced by the divine male energy of the White Spring, at the foot of the Tor. Many centuries ago the Red Spring would have stained the ground along its path a rich red from the iron, and the White Spring was a calcium stained gully, white from its waters. Our ancestors would have seen a very different landscape here, and the red and white land, together with the waters, would have created an evocative atmosphere of strangeness and awe, visibly demonstrating the ancient pagan 'mysteries'. Now the land is tamer, and its sacredness is shown by the care that people give to this place, as well as the ever present 'feeling' that so many experience. I come to the Well and feel the Great Mother all around. I meditate and feel the earth energies, the spirit of earth, rising up from the depths, and to me it is the Goddess breathing in and out, in and out.

The Goddess here has many aspects and names, which have surely been worshipped and invoked here by priestesses and witches like myself for thousands of years. In the ancient past, like today, I believe She was worshipped openly and proudly here, but I do not believe that She was forgotten during the years of Christian power, merely remembered secretly, and honoured by her ancient name of Brigid, converted from Goddess to the midwife of Christ. While also honoured at Bride's Mound, I feel She is also present at Chalice Well, the Red Spring being a source of feminine power. Brigid's legendary care for women and childbirth, attests to this. Other Goddess aspects I feel here include Creiddyled or Cordelia, a maiden Goddess of flora and fauna

on your way in

drink the water from the Lion's Head

the flowform

children love the water

relaxing in the garden

the lower lawn on Companions' Day, seen from the top of the flowform 55

lighting the fire at the winter solstice

monks debating in the Cress Field

waterfall candlelit for Hallowe'en

monks creating a peace mandala

light phenomenon at the Lion's Head

view of Glastonbury Tor from the top of the meadow

for whom it is said the local god Gwyn ap Nudd battles Gwythr each Beltane (1st May). And of course The Lady of the Lake, whether goddess or priestess, can also be felt here. A guardian of the ancient treasures of Britain, Her connection with the sacred waters position Her as a caretaker of the soul, as well as Otherworldly guide. In my experience this priestessly energy is still available to assist in magics, especially those relating to our relationship with this sacred site. Now the water that surrounded Glastonbury is gone; but Her home, the Well, remains.

The sacredness of wells goes back to the pagan animistic days, when water sources were seen as each having their own deity or nymph, and gifts were left for the spirits of the place. 'Wishing' wells hark back to the old ways of asking for help from these local spirits, these 'powers of place', and giving gifts, offerings of objects, or of love and care in exchange. I feel warm inside at Chalice Well to see this tradition continue and thrive. For me it is about the maintenance of important connections between humans and other forms of intelligence and life on this beautiful planet. It is something that my soul needs, that it seems everybody needs, in one way or another, to feel whole. At the Well I feel how connected I am to life, how the seasons of the garden reflect the seasons of my moods, my dreams, my work and rest. I am sure I am not alone in that. Indeed, drinking at the lion's head, or paddling at the healing pool, I see tensions fading from the faces around me, and feel that same ease uncrease my own brow, and suddenly to be human and alive has nothing to do with my work, my worries, or anybody else's, but becomes about the simple but most important things. Being human and alive becomes about my heart beating, the clean breath in my lungs, the feel of the water cold on my feet, its sounds burbling in my ears; it's about the murmured voices of the strangers taking their socks off to paddle, about the children playing; it's about the connection I feel with my friends each feeling here they are at peace, it's about the stillness of someone sitting listening alone and barely noticed amongst the apple trees, smiling as they gaze at the sky. All of us connected by the sensuality of living, and by the sacredness of this very special place.

By many, Chalice Hill and the Tor are considered a faery place, a gateway to the Celtic Otherworld. The Otherworld is the roots, and in many ways the womb of the earth, from which the Celtic peoples have always drawn spiritual nourishment. In my experience Chalice Well functions as a gate to this realm, for the spiritual nourishment of all. The faery folk, while not always adhering to human agendas, are a separate form of intelligence on the land, and much more connected to 'source' than humans. They have often been our friends, encouraging the interchange of energy and inspiration, as well as assisting in healing both land and people. I feel honoured by feeling their presence at the Well. Faery places, like Avalon, have always been known as areas where the veils of perception become thin, and there is much opportunity for exchange and change. In my meditations at the Well I feel this place to be just that, a place where many walks of life come together and are refreshed, via the Otherworld energies. The ancient local deity Gywn ap Nudd is the guardian of the Otherworld. In my opinion His presence is most discernable at Beltane and Samhain, the Celtic new year on the 31st October, when traditionally he rides out for the 'wild hunt' to lead the spirits of the dead to his Otherworld realm. This is another important aspect of Chalice Well, a physical site of 'source' from which life comes, but also to which life returns.

However, the faeries are not our only friends at the Well. The powerful earth energies here, together with the beautiful work of the gardeners, has led this place to be a place of particularly responsive devas, and plant spirits. In my work as a flower essence maker and practitioner, I have learnt how effective their assistance can be. This is due to their great love and kindness in assisting the healing and development of their human neighbours. The plant spirits at the Well assist me in many ways. They are an essential component of the good effects that being in nature has on our human systems, not only in the beauty they create, but also energetically. All things in existence have an energetic pattern and vibrational rate. It is these energetic 'signatures', held in water that make flower essences, but they don't have to be preserved in this way to benefit humans. Simply being near a plant or tree will effect our energy patterns, encouraging health and well-being, and imbuing our spirits with the spiritual and energetic qualities of the plant. Sometimes these energy patterns relate to herbal uses, but often they are much more subtle and much deeper working. The uses of herbs and flower essences go back impossibly far, and are essentially the magic potions of the past. I use them today in many ways for magic and healing. At Chalice Well these plant intelligences can be contacted in meditation via the individual plant, or the even more interactive overarching 'devas' which represent them, and help facilitate contact. In my experiences at the Well I have seen them with my inner eye as tall and slender leaf-faced beings. They have greatly helped in my education. Some of the most powerful plant spirits in the garden are those of the yew trees. Yew trees can teach us about stillness and the massive spans of time that are part of nature's rhythm, as can be seen by their meaning in the Celtic ogham, or tree alphabet. They remind me that the world is in greater hands than mine and that my perspective is limited. To one human life, the yew trees are almost immortal, but they are children compared to the ancient Red Spring, that has seen so many ages come and go.

As a witch and Celtic shaman, I feel it is my duty, like others, to perform a priestess role in this beautiful place, by the giving of offerings and care for the Well and garden, but also by communing and communicating with the other forms of intelligence that dwell here. In ancient times, people felt much closer to the earth and to spirit, and this encouraged a flow of energy and wisdom, of inspiration, *'awen'* which greatly benefited the human race as well as maintaining a holistic relationship with our environment. This connection has always been available to all people, but is much neglected in modern society. Yet the earth, and its other inhabitants, need conscientious human contact as much as we need them. Chalice Well is a perfect place to practice this connection, and it is my feeling that the spiritual intelligences that dwell here are often more cooperative than those in more neglected areas of this earth. The spirits here provide not only healing assistance, but are also helpful when learning and developing spiritual connection. I feel the spirits here are glad to provide a safe space for inner and spiritual exploration, and this connection can be developed by all who come here.

Facet Eight
Geomancy:
Dowsing at Chalice Well
by Sig Lonegren

Geomancy literally means "Earth Divination." Until the Protestant Reformation. European Geomancers located, oriented and over-saw the construction of sacred sites and also located and psychically cleaned secular sites, like people's homes as well. In Chalice Well, a geomancer can dowse where important power centres are located that will enhance the chances of pilgrims and other seekers making spiritual connection.

There's one immediate problem when one dares to write about geomancy and dowsed Earth Energies in sacred space. I call it "Sig's Hypothesis Number One - Even if they had the same teacher, no two dowsers will probably ever find the exactly the same thing when dowsing for intangible targets in sacred space." This is certainly true in Chalice Well.

We all "see" the spiritual realms differently – that's why there are Christians, Moslems, Jews, Hindus, Pagans, Buddhists and Native Americans, each with their different visions of the spiritual realms. Within Christianity, while all followers of that path have Christ as their focus, there are Anglicans, Greek Orthodox, Presbyterians, Methodists, Jehovah's Witnesses, Roman Catholics, etc. etc. – we all see the Numinous/God/Goddess differently. Likewise, In Chalice Well, each of us might benefit from being in different places to experience the Spiritual.

I had assumed that most would agree that the big power centre in the Gardens is at the Well Head. Several years ago, I was teaching a workshop in the Meeting Room, and asked my students to go in their mind's eye to their two favourites places in the garden, then to break into

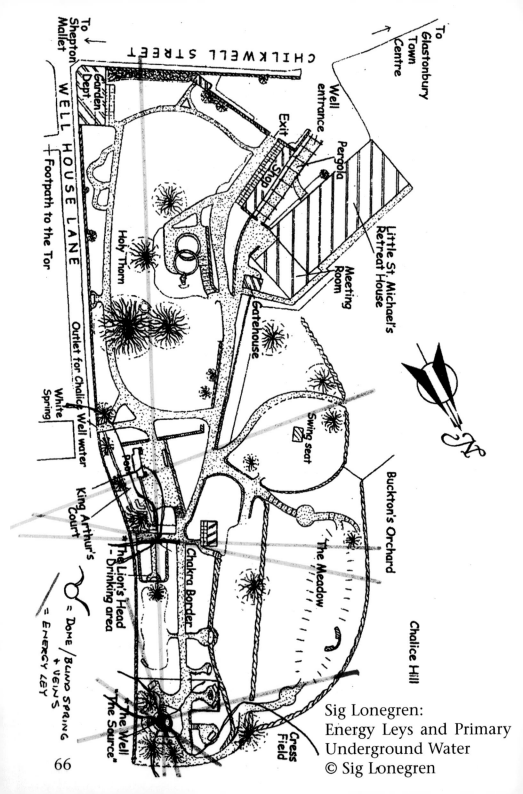

Sig Lonegren:
Energy Leys and Primary
Underground Water
© Sig Lonegren

66

groups of two and go out to these places and dowse each other's auras. That evening after closing time, I gave them a simple ceremony for each of them to do, and asked them to go to the spot where their aura had been most expanded, and do their ceremony there.

I went to the Well Head for mine. No one else was there!

Clearly, there are as many different interpretations of the energies as there are dowsers. In dowsing, it's a bit like the three blind men and the elephant. They each "saw" and described different part of that enormous animal. I want to give you more evidence of this by discussing how three experienced dowsers "see" the energies within the Chalice Well Garden. I would like to begin with how I have dowsed the energies at the Well, followed by dowser Hamish Miller, author (along with Paul Broadhurst) of "The Sun and the Serpent" who sees what he calls the Michael and Mary Lines, and finally the Michael and Mary Lines as dowsed by local dowser Tony Kentish.

I was taught to dowse for energy leys (six to eight foot wide beams of yang energy that run in straight lines and many times – but not always – run concurrently with, Alfred Watkins' leys). Energy leys cross at power centres over underground domes (a.k.a. blind springs) or veins of primary water which are the yin side of the energy circuit. (Sig Lonegren. 2004. *Spiritual Dowsing*. Bloomington, Indiana, USA: Author House. ISBN 1-4184-5888-0)

November 12, 1996 will always live in my heart. On that day Sue Barnet and I were working on a project (that we have not yet finished) to dowse the energy leys of Glastonbury. On that day, we were dowsing Chalice Well. Also on that day, I first saw Karin, my wife-to-be, across the well head!

On that day, Sue and I mapped the leys and underground water that we found in the Chalice Well gardens, and they, along with various spots I would call

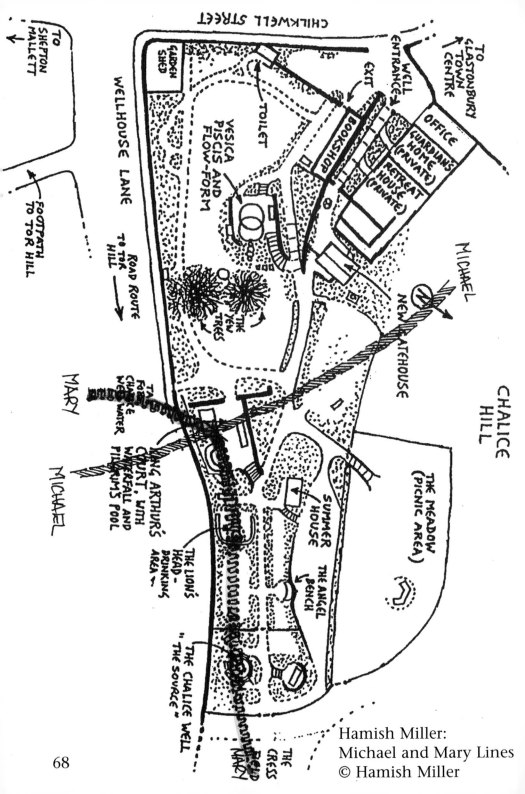

Hamish Miller:
Michael and Mary Lines
© Hamish Miller

68

"power centres", are reproduced on the map opposite. Note that for me, the three major crossings of energy leys are at the well head, at the top of the water falls, and in Arthur's Court. This is how this blind man/dowser sees the energetic sacred space elephant.

Master Dowser Hamish Miller sees the Earth Energy Elephant quite differently. He began by dowsing for John Michell's Michael Line, a wide alignment of sites that run diagonally through England, from St. Michael's Mount in Cornwall, up through other Michael points, including the Tor and up through Avebury to Bury St. Edmunds and beyond. Instead of a straight line, Hamish dowsed a snaking one he called the Michael Line (yang), and then, he discovered a second (yin) line that intertwines with it that he called the Mary Line. (Paul Broadhurst & Hamish Miller. 2003. *The Sun and the Serpent*, Launceston, Cornwall: Mythos. ISBN 0-95151-831-3) It reminds me of the Ida and Pingala, the kundalini serpents that run up the shushima of John Michell's straight Michael Line, a geomantic corridor, which would be the spine itself. At Chalice Well, he finds these two lines crossing at the top of the rectangular pool in Arthur's Court where I had found one of my power centres.

Tony Kennish has taken Hamish's work to heart, and, over the years, has done a considerable amount of dowsing of the Michael and Mary Lines here in Glastonbury. (Anthony Kennish. 2002/03. *The Glastonbury Chronicles: A New Study and Dowsed maps of the Earth Energies of Glastonbury*. Self Published.) Notice how even though he was dowsing for the same thing as Hamish – the Michael Line (perpendicular on the map) and the Mary Line (running horizontally on the map) - he not only finds the Mary line following a path through the entire length of the garden, but the Michael Line is now two lines! (Notice that Tony also finds a crossing of the Michael and Mary Lines in Arthur's Court.

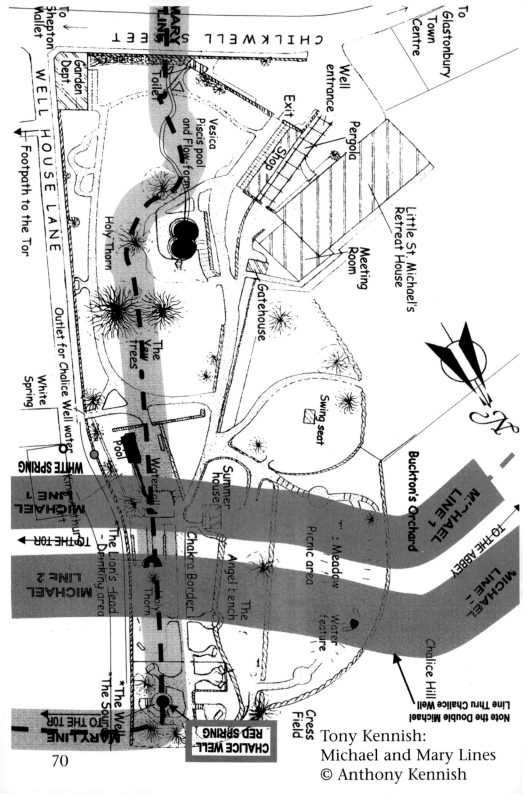

Tony Kennish:
Michael and Mary Lines
© Anthony Kennish

70

Conclusion

No one is right or wrong here, but this is a strong demonstration of how three dowsing geomancers – Hamish Miller, Tony Kennish and Sig Lonegren, see the Earth Energies differently at Chalice Well, yet manage to share one power centre in common. These are good examples of the blind men looking at the elephant. It is equally certain that some readers will feel that other places – unmarked on these maps – are important power places as well – each of us "sees" intangible targets differently. While this is anathema to science, it is the way it is when one is dealing with the spiritual realms.

Facet Nine

 ## Being a Gatehouse Volunteer
by Jen Wakefield

I have been volunteering in the gatehouse for eight years, doing at least two shifts per week often more during the summer. In the last three years I have covered a lot of the Sunday gatehouse as it is the most difficult day for volunteers to commit to. I have also have been an office volunteer, and presently I am in the shop in the same context, but the gatehouse stays firmly at the top of my list as the best place to be! Shifts are two hours only, and tea and biscuits are available.

Why do I give so much of my time to the Well?

Because I care deeply for it; sometimes I think it is a bit like a love affair, at other times when I feel the joy and peacefulness that Chalice Well can be so good at, I feel blessed to have been lucky enough to find it, and encompass it, as part as my healing journey.

I enjoy the gatehouse because however I feel when I arrive, I always feel better when I leave!! I did not question why for ages until one day someone asked me, and I thought about it at length. When I sit on the gate I am very aware that I am the visitor's first experience of Chalice Well, so therefore it is important to me that I project a positive, loving and helpful energy; in doing this, it becomes real and mostly I go home feeling great. So perhaps it is true that what you give out you get back ten fold, or is it in service there is true joy? Whatever the reason I give thanks to have been guided to Chalice Well.

Over the years I have repeatedly witnessed the instantaneous transformation that Chalice Well is capable of; usually it is first timers who go in grey-faced and miserable and who turn up at the gate sometimes only a very short time later shining and happy, visibly transformed, telling me how amazing they feel, and what a wonderful garden it is. Sometimes they have many questions, other times they just need to express their joy. Each time this happens it reinforces my respect and love for Chalice Well. I have to say "awesome" in the very truest sense of the word.

I also hear the sad stories that people tell me and have been moved to tears many times. At these times the Well seems to be able to give solace and support them in their grief. I have heard it described as being like a salve for the mind that helps to dull the pain of the grief. I have heard the most moving stories of the physical healings that happen to people who have contact with the garden and /or drink the water. Over the years that I have been in the gatehouse it probably runs past the hundred, everything from warts dropping off, to cancer being cured.

I particularly recall one American lady who had brought her mother the previous year, who had lung cancer. When she got home and went to see her physician the next x-rays were clear, there was no cancer anywhere in her body. My favourite is probably the lady who sat in the healing pool asking for her infertility problem to be overcome, who had twins, precisely ten months later. This perhaps serves to remind us to remember only to ask what we really want!!!!?

I really enjoy meeting and talking to the world-wide Chalice Well family, as the Companions seem to be calling themselves now. I do not know quite when this phrase was coined but it is great, and now when I renew companion-ships I do say, "Welcome to the family!" We are over three thousand, and increasing most years; most of these folk keeping Chalice Well close to their hearts, which I am sure helps our beloved Well and garden to thrive.

So is it any wonder that I feel privileged and honoured to be able to serve at Chalice Well, even when it is difficult, say for example on very hot days when it is really busy, and most people are feeling too hot, and maybe a bit " tetchy", and they have to wait to get in, the frustration and irritation generally just rolls away.

The Well has her moods, everything and beyond the human spectrum. It is the days when chaos seems to try and rule, that really presses my buttons; I drop things, the till won't open when it should, the telephone will not work, and the interaction with the public seems slightly adrift, misunderstandings abound! I try to rise above with humour. It usually works.

When I am away, travelling or visiting I can just close my eyes and visualise myself sitting in the gatehouse. I turn round in my chair with my back to the admissions hatch, on my left is the massive mother beech whispering to all who will listen, for me she is the guardian to the entrance and I always say "hello" and I usually tell her my troubles! I turn gently right and directly in my view are the two powerful yews, the gap between them in my mind creates a magical doorway to the essence of Chalice Well. Whenever I am on the gate duty I always, no matter how busy it is try to get five minutes just to absorb their precious energies. Then I gently start turning my chair fully to the right and gradually the vesica flowform comes into view. The water here being asked to make spirals and almost turn somersaults, I love to sit and listen to this tumbling; it is almost as if the water is laughing. Perhaps this is why the vesica pool is such a favourite with the children who visit? Then I turn fully to the front and I have the beautiful gateway and above that a stunning view over the Somerset levels.

I hope your visits to Chalice Well gives you joy, and you leave with a bit more love in your heart.

The Upper Room replicating how WTP "saw" the venue for the Last Supper. Note the light which shines perpetually in the west window.

Facet Ten

On Being A Trustee
by Roy Procter

What is a Trustee? Trustees are volunteers, in fact they are prevented by law from receiving any payment, other than out of pocket expenses. They are responsible for overseeing that a Charity operates in accordance with the objects of its governing document, and they are also personally responsible, without limit, for its financial affairs. Their conduct and responsibilities are governed by Charity Law.

I have been a Trustee of the Chalice Well Trust since 1991 so have seen many changes and developments. My connection with the place developed over many years.

My wife, Ann, and I read Tudor Pole's books with great interest. We had met him briefly in the 1960's, but our first visit to Glastonbury was not until the early 70's. We attended a meeting of the Wrekin Trust, of which we were long standing members, in Glastonbury Town Hall. We wanted to visit the Chalice Well and see the Upper Room of which we had read so much, but did not know how to go about obtaining access to this very special place. Sir George Trevellyan provided us with an introduction. So we marched off to the Well and were met by the Warden, John Simmons. The introduction had the desired effect and we were led up to the Upper Room forthwith.

We were both immediately aware of the amazing 'ambience' of this room and soaked this up in silence. In those days, the room was divided by a low wooden rail and a gauze curtain. Behind the curtain the table was set with the chairs and utensils that we had read about, being TP's recreation of his vision of the setting for the Last Supper. We felt that this arrangement significantly added to the magic of the room. At the other end of the room I came upon a small table in a window niche. I was astonished to find the Blue Bowl there in its open case! The 'energy', or whatever, that seemed to emanate from it was amazing and very powerful. In fact I can sense this again as I write this thirty years later. Chalice Well and the Upper Room are certainly the most powerful places I had ever visited, and so they still are.

So we were 'hooked', and became Companions, but did not visit the Well much, as we lived in Surrey. In 1984 a change of job provided the opportunity to settle near Glastonbury and to visit the Well more often. Shortly after my retirement from full time employment in 1991 our old friend Marigold, a current Trustee, phoned. Without any preliminaries she asked if I would become a Trustee of the Well with a view to taking over as Chairman! After I had recovered from the shock, she explained that the then Chairman, Lord Grey, in post since the Trust was formed in 1959, was ageing and succession was not being addressed. Many of the other Trustees were also getting older and did not live locally. The following Companions' day Ann and I met Lord Grey in the garden shelter. He talked about his war experiences for some time and then said "You'll do", and walked off. I hardly said a word! We had a strong feeling that really I was being assessed by TP himself. And so I was invited to become a Trustee.

There were then nine Trustees. Four lived locally, Lord Grey lived near Manchester, and the others lived in the London area. They only met four times a year. At these meetings the Trustees had very little influence as the Warden decided everything. Any questioning usually resulted in us being told that he had already agreed the matter with the Chairman by telephone.

In 1993 the other Trustees persuaded Lord Grey to step down and I was unanimously asked to take on the Chairmanship, and I do not think the Warden was happy with a new broom! I was not sure that we were in compliance with our obligations under the law so we instigated a 'Legal Audit' of our operations. An independent solicitor reviewed our affairs and identified a number of shortcomings in our procedures, which we immediately rectified. We found that the Chalice Well property had been purchased in pieces at various times. The deeds for each piece were in the names of different Trustees long since departed. So the Trustees become a corporate body so that all land and other assets could be in the name of that body. Negotiations with the Charity Commission took a year!

The financial reporting and controls needed to be overhauled and made more transparent. In this we were lucky to recruit Barry Taylor, with his financial expertise, as a new Trustee. Barry made many improvements in our procedures, including introducing annual budgets and associated financial monitoring. This significantly improved the ability of the Trustees to work with the staff to better advantage.

Eventually the Warden decided to retire so the Trustees needed to find a replacement. We advertised the post, partly because it would be difficult to get a work permit for non-EU citizens, and an eager couple from America had already applied. There were 250 applications! Forty serious ones were discussed, and we interviewed seven couples. After much more discussion the US couple was selected. It was then necessary to provide officialdom with reasons for our choice to obtain a work permit. More paperwork!

Thus Fred & Colleen Rosado took up the post. They immediately brought welcome changes: a more open atmosphere to the Well, and a more entrepreneurial approach to the finances, mainly through developments of trading through the shop.

During this period there seemed to be a possibility of the White Spring becoming available. We investigated in considerable detail the possibilities of acquisition with the intention of preserving the spring as a spiritual venue. Structural surveys were not particularly encouraging. Trustee John Rowntree worked on this with great diligence, but it was not possible to arrive at any sound arrangement.

As a result of the Rosados' expansion of activities in the shop, more space was required. More activity in the shop made it difficult for one volunteer to operate the shop sales, and take the entrance money from visitors. So a new gate house was built, with all that this entailed in design, planning permission, reworking of the entrance way, car parking etc. This was a major project for all concerned. In retrospect this was clearly a very beneficial change, providing a better reception for visitors.

The Rosados efforts were increasing the occupancy rate of the Retreat House. It became clear that there was not enough 'social space' in relation to bedroom accommodation. A conservatory over the small courtyard beyond the dining room was considered, various other schemes were investigated, but none seemed to be satisfactory physically or financially at that stage.

In 1998 the Rosados fell out with each other. They had given great service by opening up and improving the work of the Trust and its finances in many ways. The Trustees felt that a period of good management and better administration was required for consolidation before undertaking further developments.

We wished to avoid the work overload involved in advertising for new Wardens. Fortunately, while turning out old scrap paper, a letter responding to the advertisement of 3 years ago emerged. It was from Michael and Lynne Orchard. On the previous occasion we would have seriously considered their application, but they withdrew due to being in India at interviewing time. They were contacted, expressed great interest in the position this time, and were invited for interview. In short order it was agreed unanimously that the Orchards be appointed. Is this 'coincidence' the way spirit works?

We were all saddened when one of our most stalwart Trustees, John Rowntree, became seriously ill and died. However he left us a significant legacy with provision that it be used for a major capital project. It was clear what he had in mind: John had masterminded the investigations into possible extensions over the courtyard by the Retreat House: he was obviously providing the financial incentive for us to do something. Companion Wilf Burton was engaged to propose a suitable scheme and planning permission was obtained. The result was the present Meeting Room. The quotations for building were significantly greater than envisaged. So we had to balance the use of some of our investments, and the running costs involved, against projected revenue. It felt like a very big decision! Eventually we went ahead. Subsequent events have shown that we were right: the room is well used and is more than viable financially

Unexpected expenses gave us more worries. Obligatory archaeology cost us £1800. Then there was a VAT inspection. To our astonishment they said that we owed £12,000 for building the new Meeting Room. We had investigated this and been told that a charity was not liable. A different inspector deemed otherwise. A very competent VAT consultant could make no headway on our behalf, so we had to pay up.

I have set out some of the main matters that have been addressed by the Trustees. But in addition to these more major considerations, there is mundane monitoring of every day matters. During my time as chairman, there has been a steady turnover of Trustees, as those who feel that they have done enough are replaced by newcomers. We have encouraged replacements living in the local community rather than far away. This enables Trustees to be in closer touch and readily available to support the staff, resulting in better ability to make the right policy decisions when required. They are also available at short notice for checking invoices, signing cheques and giving guidance, or authorising actions outside the remit of staff members. Much time and effort is given to producing an annual budget and monitoring the management, and financial reports of progress throughout the year.

The Trustees are responsible in Law to the Charity Commission for the conduct of the Trust. There has been a huge increase in legislation over the last few years. Employment laws have been introduced that require a great increase of paperwork to engage staff. Staff cannot now be dismissed without following a lengthy and set procedure, with the threat of being sued for wrongful dismissal if not done correctly. Nobody is expected to take responsibility for their own accident, hence the proliferation of notices all over the gardens. The Charity Commission now expect us to have written policy documents for a very wide range of matters. These include forward policy plans, financial risk assessments, a whole range of health and safety risk assessments, staff policies, policies for the disabled, policies for procedure in certain events etc. All these matters occupy very significant amount of staff time (and hence expense), as well as attention by the Trustees. Thus it is now more important than ever that the Board of Trustees is composed of competent people who, between them, provide a mix of skills and experience. And as the main work of the Trust is to encourage spiritual awareness, Trustees also need to be well into their own spiritual journey. It is not easy to find such people who are also able to give the time and attention necessary to Trusteeship.

At the beginning of 2001 I handed over the chairmanship to Alan Gloak while remaining on the Board. He soon became Mayor of Glastonbury, and subsequently Chairman of the Somerset County Council.

He resigned in early 2005 to be replaced by Kyrin Singleton. In mid-2005 the Guardians, Lynne and Michael Orchard, resigned suddenly and reported sick. Kyrin also resigned due to ill health, and I was asked to resume the chairmanship, with co-chair Tyna Redpath, for a limited period while the Trust reorganised itself.

One thing is now clear. Wardens become influenced by the powerful energies of the Well and, in time, become very possessive of the place. This leads to difficulties with the Trustees. So, we are now trying a different staff set up with the coordinator/manager living off the premises. The relationship between Trustees, who have all the responsibility, and the managers who must be left to manage, is tricky. I will be resigning from the board in mid-2006. and will be interested to see how things develop. Although there have been some difficult times and much hard work. there have been several significant advances, and I have enjoyed my fourteen years of service to this magical place.

Facet Eleven

From the Staff Who Work at the Well

Currently, there are fourteen members of staff at the Chalice Well, full and part-time. But this number could be misleading, as we could not continue to function without our five self-employed assistants plus our many loyal volunteers. We divide into four main groups: those concerned with the garden and with maintenance; those who work in the office; those who are responsible for housekeeping; and those who work in the shop.

Running the Chalice Well is a seven days a week, 365 days a year operation with all the complexities that belong to a business operating in the modern world. We have to be prepared to work flexible hours and have a member of staff on site at all times; so one of our number lives in a cottage next to the office. Between us we manage two retreat houses that can accommodate up to sixteen guests a night, keep open the only public garden in Glastonbury (currently receiving over 40,000 visitors a year), hire out a meeting room for workshops, seminars, talks and meetings, run a shop and mail order, maintain a membership of over 3,000 Companions, produce newsletters, run two websites, generate publicity, administrate a charitable trust, run retreats and organise up to twenty events a year, including concerts and ceremonies that can involve up to five hundred participants. Sometimes it feels like the health and safety issues alone require a full time member of staff!

We find multi-tasking and prioritisation are necessities; patience, good humour and the ability to delegate are absolutely essential. We also need to know each others strengths and weaknesses and cover for each other whenever necessary. But when all is said and done our aim is to provide an unspoilt experience of the Chalice Well for our Companions and visitors.

At the start of each day, we come together to discuss what is on the agenda, and organise ourselves to deal with the tasks and any issues that may arise. The weekly staff meeting is a more in-depth affair where we discuss longer term issues, such as upcoming events. Every staff member is free to share their ideas and suggestions; and in some instances, such as the events, we are free to ,volunteer ourselves as little or as much, as we wish. Each person tends to get more involved in the events that are close to their heart.

"As a new member of staff," wrote Jill Osborne, "my initial thoughts as I walked through the door on my first day were that I wasn't aware of the amount and variety of tasks required to run the office and gardens. I was pleasantly surprised to hear about the staff circle meetings and that everyone was actively involved in the organisation and could be part of the decision making. This was an alien concept to me and was most welcome."

At times, working in the office can be an intense experience. (This is where the good humour comes in handy!) In one desperate scenario: the phones are ringing; guests are arriving and need to be shown in; there is an emergency call from the volunteer in the gatehous;, a knock on the door (delivery to be checked off); a group leader requires assistance in the Meeting Room; the shop needs an item of stock; and you are the only person in the office. You then have your own area of responsibility to cover: letters to write, orders to make, papers to file and the letters have to be franked before the postman arrives. Sometimes it feels as though to provide the peace and tranquillity that are present in the gardens, all the energy, stress and bother of the world is left at the entrance and finds its way into the office!

The shop is an important part of the service we provide to the visitor to the well. We are aware that after a visit to the garden, people want to take something away, however small, that reconnects them to the well and reminds them of their experience. For this reason, we try to stock in our little shop items that are often unique, unavailable elsewhere, and have the quality of the gardens.

"As a member of staff," said Nicholas Mann, the Companion Registrar, "I don't enjoy the multi-tasking and the constant interruptions to my work. But it's just something I get used to and it's made worthwhile by the rewards. Where else could I work and hear people comment that what we have made available to them has touched them in some way, has opened their hearts, even healed them? The garden is like a temple: I enter at the gates, leave the world behind; work my way through the succession of spaces – each like a vestibule – until I reach the sanctuary itself, at the wellhead. And, most wonderfully, it is a natural temple, sanctified by the devas, the birdsong, the sun and wind, the elements themselves. There is nothing between me, the world and its soul. When I can find those moments - especially at an event or a ceremony - when our circle joins with the circle of earth, with the soul of all beings, then I feel good being in service here at the Well - the springs of Avalon."

The theme of service is very strong for all those who give their time and energy to the Well. "It's about giving oneself freely, unreservedly and without expectations, or even without recognition," said Simon Wardle, the office administrator. "I think we often do that unconsciously, without thinking about it, here at the Well. I have worked at Chalice Well longer than in any other place, and it is rewarding, challenging, uncomfortable, and pushes me to the limits. The challenge is that it is so easy to get absorbed and sucked into everything that goes on at the Well but one has to try not to put one's personality into it. I think we get better with practice. The Well is a forgiving place."

Simon also commented on the changes that inevitably happen to all those who work at the Well. "People move on when the Well has served its purpose for each individual. There will be a time when it's right for me to move on; it feels right to be here at the moment. I hope we will try not to shape the Well in any unnatural way. We are superfluous, the Well doesn't need us. It's humbling to remember that."

"I am just one in a long line of gardeners," said Ark Redwood, the head gardener, also addressing this theme. "We have all added to the Garden. We are all earth-weavers. I have a commitment to be here for twenty years, or even longer; but, if I'm not supposed to, then that is OK too. Every time a long-living plant is planted there is a good feeling about giving pleasure to people for years to come. I am proud to be here to enhance people's perception of the nature realm. I am honoured to work with that realm in a place where such co-creation, such earth-weaving, is possible."

"When I think about service and the Well," said Natasha Wardle, the shop manager, "something inside me unravels and I feel a welling up of emotion – not in a bad way, but in an exquisite way. Being here at the Well is about being connected to the deepest expression of Truth. I live for that. It's not just about the place, or the Well, in the physical sense, it's about the Source of the Well, and how that source finds expression, or is given expression, in and through us. I have been here now five years, and I know that I am not the same person who came. It has changed me without any effort on my part. It has changed how I think, how I feel, how I respond to situations, and I love that."

As is clear from these remarks, the Well takes on a shape, a presence, even a personality in its own right with those who develop a relationship with it over time. The encounter with this being is intimate, personal and, like any relationship, it can be unpredictable and challenging. It is, above all, a spiritual encounter. "I feel privileged to be here; even when it is uncomfortable" said the weekend manager, summing it all up. "The Well engages every part of me. I feel my soul is doing a dance with the soul of the Well. I feel a deep connection with the Well that touches me and makes me want to give everything. The flip side is when it doesn't all meet, and it doesn't all dance. It is such a huge learning curve. It's about forgetting me and remembering the Eternal Soul."

Facet Twelve
Staying at Chalice Well and Running Courses
by Sarah Stewart

"I feel as though I have come home."

Imagine prairies as far as the eye can see, big sky country, coulees and sage brush; where an old house means it was built in the 1940's; where the myths and legends and the story of the landscape is not your own but belonging to another people who lived on the land for millennia – while you have belonged but three generations. There are no gardens, just backyards, where vegetables are grown, and a few hardy flowers if you are lucky, and as long as plants are started in pots in the house because of the frost.

Canadian women from such landscapes have accompanied me on many spiritual journeys to Glastonbury where we have stayed at Chalice Well. It was often their first journey to England. Pat said, "All those years studying English Literature and poetry and I never had a picture in my head of what is a spring, a hawthorn, a rose, hedgerow or yew tree, and now I am enriched. This place has given me back my imagination." Barbara left England when she was 10. I told her in our pre-meeting in Canada that even though I had left England to live in Canada, almost 30 years ago, I never truly felt connected to the Earth unless I was home, and to me home's centre was the Chalice Well Garden. After we arrived in Chalice Well, on the second day, she confided to me that what I had said, she had dismissed and 'pooh-poohed'. "But now I know exactly what you mean because I feel it too." "It's as though I have connected with our ancestral spirits," said another. "We belong. I feel as though I have come home."

The back door to Little St Michael's, the retreat house at Chalice Well, was like a swing door in a western saloon in constant use, as women would go into the garden, come back in to tell what they had seen, and minutes later, were magnetised outside again. Many found the energies of the town of Glastonbury overpowering and exhausting at first but once they came back to the Garden felt instantly refreshed and at peace.

"Chalice Well was a very powerful experience; a whole new world opened for me. I began to explore what it means to be truly and wholly human. Before I came on this journey I had found a drawing of the Vesica Piscis and was very attracted to it. I kept it and began using it in stencilling and cross-stitch. On arrival at Chalice Well I saw the same Viscia Piscis that I had been copying all winter. I felt a huge sense of wonder to have been led to this very place by a series of 'coincidences'. It is a powerful spiritual place for me, a cathartic one, where the air itself is a presence." Margaret B. Canada.

My journeys were called 'Healing Holidays'. And maybe that is why so many women who came with me had sorrows and sadness to heal, wounded and broken hearts from a death, divorce, loss of children, or loss of love. What is the magic of the garden today? How does it support us? For all of us it was a place of healing our hurts and becoming ready to forgive and let go of pain. One woman said, "I can't forgive my father. He deserted me in so many ways. I never knew him." In the sunlit meadow in the Garden we explored what forgiveness really means when we forgive ourselves, and forgive others, and how it gives us back our freedom and our power. I led a guided meditation with the only background sound being bees buzzing. We asked that if we could not forgive then perhaps we could come to a place where we were willing to forgive. A fire engine went by with sirens blaring, then trucks rumbled by on the road below. I soldiered on, thinking they will have lost their concentration and it is not going to work. When they came out of meditation they looked like awakened sleepers. I mentioned all the disturbances and asked if they were able to meditate in spite of them. They looked at me perplexed. They had not heard a thing. Their faces were suffused with peace. We decided to finish up by chanting OM. After a few moments, the sheep nearby started to loudly join in with us. We could not carry on for long because we were laughing so hard with joy. Women who came on this journey and quest were at mid-life, ready to reflect on how far they had come and envision their path ahead. Despite years of opportunities denied their own mothers, there was still a feeling of being less than, of playing a role rather than being an individual, woman the supporter and not a creative force in life. In the Garden we experienced many shifts of perspective about our own power as women, as we named the Divine in feminine terms often for the very first time. Yet sometimes this made participants feel afraid.

"What if we get struck by lightning?" said one in all seriousness. "What if this is wrong?" Becoming aware of the strong energies in the Garden at first created a sense of great unease. A sacred place like Chalice Well gives us the gift of reflection. Like looking into a mirror, we see what is inside ourselves. Often the first emotion on a spiritual quest is fear. Through gently being in this sacred place and with the support of the other women, fears were faced and overcome.

The Vesica Piscis symbolized, for us, the meaning of the Garden. It is the balance of the male and female energies. The interlinking circles form an opening, an almond like the birth canal into this life, and the doorway out. This feminine symbol is crossed with the sword, a masculine symbol, that shows the two polarities of our being brought into balance. By honouring our femininity and also our masculine energies, we brought ourselves into harmony and to a place of peace.

The energies of Chalice Well give to us, but can we receive? Can we translate our visions, hopes and dreams into action in the world? Here many participants had that 'Aha' moment, when they realised the power of women as a creative force in the world. This knowing was not as a result of what we did in ritual, ceremony, prayer or song but these outwardly manifested the action of the Garden on our inner beings, the 'loci spiritus' that communicated with us by our just being and dreaming there. We came to realise that love is a state of being, not a feeling or an emotion. It is the peaceful relationship with the self, and it was the gift of the Garden to us. In the evenings, after visitors had gone, we were free to enjoy the Garden alone because we were staying at Little St. Michael's. The flowers seemed to exude a silvery light, the moon shone and we danced under the yew trees in our bare feet. Linda felt as though she had totally accepted her body and her life through becoming grounded in the earth. She felt she had struggled from birth to accept her existence but now she felt, "I have a right to be born and a right to be here."

Being able to stay in the Garden at Little St Michael's was a great gift. The retreat house is alive with energy. Powerful leylines run through the house and we were told residents have many strange experiences. "It's only fair to warn you," the Guardian told us, "you might see or hear something in the night." This was to two of us staying in the bedroom that used to be Wellesley Tudor Pole's study. 'But don't be scared." We slept soundly however. The only strange experiences we had were an infusion of creative and physical energy.

The Guardian also told us a powerful ley line ran through the kitchen, right through the sink, and if we did not wash and put away the dishes at night we would not sleep well! Afterwards we wondered if this was a ploy to make sure we cleaned up, and I admit we did not do them one night and.....we did not sleep well! The main room has a huge stone nook where the fireplace once was but now with a sofa in it. We loved talking and having workshops here because of the energy, taking it in turns to sit in the powerful fireplace. The Upper Room was often visited for silent thoughts, and seemed full of hidden companions. With no radio, telephone, television, stone flagged floors and simple rooms, and heavy wooden antique furniture, we stepped back to the past and out of our everyday lives. The library afforded intriguing reading matter.

After receiving so much, we returned gifts to the Garden which were our songs at the Well Head. And in this magical garden, coloured like a butterfly's wing, one summer's evening, we danced on the lawn as we sang. Marie had gathered convolvulus vines from the hedgerows and she made crowns for us. Afterwards we could not bear to take them off, and we went into town for supper with them on our heads. We were middle-aged women, bankers, academics, teachers, but we sang through the town with flowers in our hair, feeling like nymphs.

"When I think of England there are three places that are the centre of everything; the Abbey, Chalice Well Garden and the Tor. They remind me of a song we used to sing at Church camp when I was growing up. "Take off your shoes. You're walking on Holy Ground." Sara C. Canada

One woman said, when she came back to Canada, "Whenever I feel overwhelmed, am struggling, or just want to feel that state of peace, I just have to close my eyes and I am there."

(All names have been altered to protect privacy.)

Facet Thirteen

Views From "Across the Pond"
from Michael Calabrese and friends

For Pagan and Christian alike, Chalice Well is a place that is woven into the dearest myths of our culture: the resting place of the cup of Christ; the home of Priestesses of the Well at the foot of Tor in countless stories; a sacred spot tied to the legends of Arthur and his single, shining moment. All of these form our images of what once was. In reality, *what was* - lays about twelve feet below the ground, and what is – is all around us within the gardens. News that Chalice Well is in the here and the now – that Avalon is not lost in the mists of the past can be disquieting. Frowns cross faces, bottoms shift uncomfortably in chairs, and that line drawn between the subjective and objective becomes blurred within those garden walls. Where that line runs when we first arrive at Chalice Well, and when we leave, can be very different places. But the Well is in the here and now, and to come to Chalice Well - is to know that the Heart of Avalon beats in our world.

For those of us who have had the wonderful fortune to come to Chalice Well, disbelief is the last thing we can feel. I don't think I know anyone who has gone there and remained unaffected. Stepping through the gates, we cross into a world we once only dreamt of. It isn't often that a cherished image - nurtured for years, survives the contact. Reality usually falls short of the mark. A day at Chalice Well, spent in its quiet and warmth, dwarfs our imaginations, and often rewrites definitions of soul and self. The hands of Divinity rise from the waters to weave their fingers through the air, the flowers, the trees and us. Those fingers can tie a heart to this place – leaving a piece of itself deeply embedded in the visitor and perhaps taking a bit in exchange. No matter the trade – we are always the richer for it, and the images we held are overwhelmed by the place that lives in the here and now.

A trip to Chalice Well for those of us on this side of The Pond, is often life altering. It's fun to dream about living in places visited while on vacation. The romance stays bright for those who will get on a plane and go back to their lives with photos and stories to tell. Chalice Well affects many Americans in a very different way, and "home" becomes the place you leave when returning to the States. Lives get changed, points of focus turn toward the water, the gardens, the Grace that lives within the grounds, and that particular spot that is yours, and yours alone – no matter how many people sit there. There is no true measure of a place in the numbers of people who say that they want to live there. There is by the numbers who do it and those who redirect their lives toward that day when they come home – and stay.

This chapter is by Companions whose lives are drawn toward Chalice Well from across The Pond. Some are determined to live close to this place of faith, magic and spirit. Others love it all the same, and would fulfill Wellesley Tudor Pole's vision of a linkage between Chalice Well and the United States, by bringing the spirit of Avalon to their country. In all, it's the love we share for this place that fills these pages.

Like many Americans, I came to Chalice Well on my first visit to Glastonbury, and like the ruins of the famous abbey and the Tor, it was one of the sites to be seen. I was there doing research, visiting places I would write about. I had some advantages - I knew I was going to see someplace special. What I knew was what was available on printed pages. I had no idea...

Walking up from the town I paused to smile at the green sign, the attractive gates and beautiful arbor. The building to my left – looked interesting. I paid a pleasant woman at the gatehouse, and stepped into a world I'd only imagined.

It was April and the West Country was exploding in a depth of color I'd never seen before. Against that backdrop, Chalice Well vibrated under the brilliant sunlight. Standing at the foot of the Vesica Pool, I found myself breathing in deeply, clearing my mind and spirit as if in preparation for a ceremony. I hadn't planned to, but it seemed natural, and entering a sacred space, I opened myself so very easily. That trip marked the first time I had ever associated any location as being a "female" place. While I'd always acknowledged the Goddess, I'd never felt her. I found peace of spirit in a place where Divinity dwells.

Walking along the pathways to sit by the Well itself, feeling that each footfall was set upon sacred ground, drinking the water from the Lion's Head – all gave me a sense of unity with the Spirit of the living world. It's a connection that never leaves me. I turned off the main path, walked down some steps and found a small quiet place where the silence was deeper - a space darkened more by shadow than shade. Sitting on the stone bench by the waterfall, I found my place in the world: King Arthur's Court - the single spot where for me, unity of body and spirit reaches its zenith. I belong there. Separation by miles and time may make me miss it, but the connection is never broken.

With each visit to the Well, the importance of this place and its impact on my life has only grown. The Upper Room within Little St. Michael's is a place of spiritual unity. Stepping through the door with the golden late afternoon light glowing through the room, the energy is there – waiting. The emotional and spiritual become substantial as every hair rises and that unity becomes a physical force.

Memories of Chalice Well have become snap-shots embedded in the spirit, images of sanctuary – a precinct where Grace lives in the world. The peace of Chalice Well is an extraordinary thing. It isn't limited to humans. Over the years I've become aware of the huge numbers of birds that come to the gardens. These wild creatures – with every reason to take flight, will sit on a branch only a foot from your head utterly without fear, and continue to sing at your approach. Once, I was sitting on the steps running along the side of the Vesica Pool when one of the resident hedgehogs came out of the bushes, walked directly to me and being curious, stuck its head into the cuff of my jeans. Satisfied that I kept a leg in there, this little creature continued its walk no more than six inches from me and then returned to the bushes. I know they are used to humans, but when was the last time you walked up to a living creature 400 times your size for a look into a cuff? Sanctuary is not ours alone.

Michael Calabrese, Ohio

Sherry Eldridge of Oklahoma writes:

Pilgrimage isn't a word that comes easily to most Americans. It's a vague notion from the past, a distant concept of a spiritual journey reserved for a few fervent souls. A pilgrimage was not on my mind during my first trip to England, not in the classic sense. Certainly it was a life dream of mine to visit 'the blessed Isles'. I had no concept of how much it would change me, nor how central Glastonbury and the Chalice Well would become.

On that first trip, the Chalice Well reached out to me long before I had any actual awareness of its existence. An acquaintance took me on a day trip to Glastonbury, this quaint medieval market town featuring so many aspects of the history and sacred myth I loved. We walked the High Street in the afternoon, climbing the Tor near the end of the day. Once upon that rise more than my visual perspective shifted. I felt the energies that crossed the mount running strong, and found myself intently drawn to a small rounded hill below, pulled so strongly I felt literally tugged at the center of my being. I asked what lay 'down there', but my companion did not know. Time was short, so we left without knowing, yet the impression remained so strong that immediately upon my next visit, I made straight for Glastonbury, finally able to follow that call back down the Tor to the entrance of what turned out to be the Chalice Well.

I spent many hours at the Well that first time, drinking it all in - refilling my glass at the Wellhead while refilling my soul in a way that defies explanation. I return now as often as possible, partly for pure pleasure, yet primarily in answer to that same initial call to the Well itself, a call that has only grown with time and each visit. Simply being in the gardens, tucked away in the cool stillness of King Arthur's Court, or enwrapped in the growing peace of the Yews, is a renewal. Whether it was initially the call of the Well to my soul, or of my soul to the Well, there is a point where the two meet. I am nourished at the very essence of being. Many have analyzed the reasons for the Well's effect. Are the profound and healing energies physical, metaphysical, spiritual, or all of the above? I'm not sure it's important to know, really. I've certainly done my own quest in attempting to understand it. What is important is the experience of it, and that it continue. That is why I became a Companion. While enjoying the benefits of Little St. Michael's, the library, and after-hours private time in the garden are priceless to me, so is the necessity that the Well be available to those who seek and feel its call. So much more flows from Chalice Well than water.

Some have called the Well and Glastonbury the heart center of the earth. I know it has become such for me, renewing and invigorating my own heart each time I connect with the energies that flow there. Chalice Well refills and recharges, allowing me to step back across the veil, bringing a little of the Light of the Well back into the World. I know I will return again, to renew once more - echoing the ageless, timeless cycle of the waters. The concept of a pilgrimage is no longer foreign to me, but integral - defined not by dogma nor distant history, but my own experience, and growing understanding of, the energies of place. Chalice Well has become a definitive spiritual pilgrimage for me - my heart's rest, my soul's home.

Jim & Kate Wolf- Pizor, California

Chalice Well has become a central focal point of Jim's spiritual meditation. I keep Well water near my personal altar as my choice of consecrated water. One of my favorite uses for Well water is as a gift to friends, marking spiritual milestones in their lives, or our relationship.

I grew up an avid reader, and the tales of Arthur and the Grail were some of my favorites. Pursuing deeper, more complex tales, led me to a rich fantasy of mythical Avalon. For me this place, which certainly would not exist on this Earth in our century, was a place of deep spiritual magic. Of course the four Queens who carry the wounded Arthur away would go to the Vale of Avalon! Only there could he be preserved and healed, to remain the protector of Britain - ready to ride again.

I came to Avalon by a remarkable chance. Business brought me to southern England. A short drive away was the West Country, gated by the venerable temple of Stonehenge and then the marvelous nooks and crannies of Somerset. Driving into Glastonbury, one perceives the Tor and the lone St. Michael's tower across the Levels. This beacon calls to us; it must be responded to, and so the journey led to Glastonbury. Changed from businessman into pilgrim, I had to climb the Tor and experience its full majesty. From the summit, one truly comprehends the mysterious Somerset Levels.

My second visit to the Well came with the blessing of accommodations inside the Gardens, at Little St. Michaels. The first night, I awakened to a bright moon shining on the mists of Avalon. Avalon is still an island - only reached by crossing those mists.

There is a spell of enchantment there. Once touched by it, one can retain that spiritual link with the sacred center, wherever life's journey takes us. While I can easily contemplate moving to Avalon, I also have its blessings here in California, many thousands of miles away. I can open my spirit and reach out to the morning mists of Avalon. I can place a drop of Well water on an object, and dedicate it to sacred purpose. Avalon nourishes me even while waiting patiently for my next reunion within its mists.

Jim Wolf-Pizor

Kate, began her long journey to the Well when she was a child.

....Of course, I did not know it at the time. Nature was alive to me and I felt a special pull to be outside by the water. The Well was first "shown" to me through the King Arthur stories, which I have read most of my life. My poor husband lives in a house with shelves and shelves of Arthur books. It was 'The Mists of Avalon' by Marion Zimmer Bradley, that felt like a call to come home to Avalon.

One wonderful day, we were on a plane to England to go home to Avalon. We reread Dion Fortune on the plane and were looking for the first sighting of the Tor. We arrived on a beautiful summer day and were met with warmth and joy. I walked into the garden and felt a jolt of recognition. It was the feeling of my grandmother's garden, a continent, and fifty years away. We walked into Little St. Michael's and found five waiting new friends, who are friends to this day.

A special memory for me was waking very early the first morning - barely dawn, and looking out of the window to be met by the mists. I wept for the utter joy and a sense of reality and wholeness. I think of that wonderful moment and am reminded of Jung's words: "Only what is really oneself has the power to heal."

We spent blissful days sketching, walking, tasting the waters and feeling at home. We held our own ritual for peace and healing over the flowing waters. The memory of that ritual is still peace-filled for me.

Prayer Beside the Well

May Avalon bring you peace.
May it be the peace of a full heart.
May Avalon bring you joy.
May it be the joy of a soft breeze at sunset.
May Avalon bring you strength.
May it be the strength of commitment and a clear Voice.
May Avalon bring you food.
May it be food for your soul from the Apple Isle.
May Avalon bring you place.
May it be a place of belonging and remembering.
May Avalon bring you home.
May it be the home of your heart.

Kate Wolf-Pizor,

Some of you may have visited Chalice Well in the past and have only now found this book. Others may have never walked the paths. It may be that this small book seemed interesting and these pages have caught your eye. A few may be thinking you would like to visit or return, others may feel you must. Some paths lead here – others lead elsewhere, but the world is like that.

For those who have just finished their visit, new feet walk the paths of Chalice Well – yours! We don't know if you will be back, although we hope you will. We don't know if you will be drawn as we are. We know that you are not unaffected – after all, you are reading this. The memory of your visit will be with you always. It may return with the sound of a bird singing somewhere near you – just over there... or perhaps it will come on the morning wind and the passing scent of the flowers. May the peace of Chalice Well live always within your heart, and return to you each time you remember the gardens at the foot of the Tor.

The gate to the outside world is just ahead. Before you leave, take one extra moment to turn and look behind you and know that wherever your Path leads you – there will never be a time when your footsteps do not join those who have walked the paths of Chalice Well. Perhaps that is what you leave behind, perhaps there is more. Whatever you take with you – will return each time you look at this book.

Appendix

1900 Restoration and cleaning of Chalice Well.

1904 Wellesley Tudor Pole's first visit to Chalice Well, situated within the grounds of the Roman Catholic Missionary College of the Sacred Heart which stood where once the Anchorage Inn had succeeded the Anchorites' huts.

1913 Alice Buckton bought Chalice Well and the surrounding grounds, including the former seminary which stood in what is now the lower gardens, Little St Michael's, Vine Cottage, May Cottage (now the office), Tor House (formerly the Anchorage Inn) and several properties in Chilkwell Street.

1919 Friends and lovers of the Well and Glastonbury presented Chalice Well with a well lid bearing a wrought iron *Vesica Piscis* pierced with a 'bleeding lance' designed by the excavator of Glastonbury Abbey, archaeologist Frederick Bligh Bond, as a Thanks-Offering for Peace.

1944 Alice Buckton died leaving all her property to the first Chalice Well Trust, naming six Trustees and outlining a very simple deed.

1959 WTP and friends, having bought the property, excluding the school, reinstated The Chalice Well Trust with a far more fullsome deed under the guidance of seven Trustees. One of them, Charles Legh Cornwall Legh, later Lord Grey of Codnor, a considerable benefactor in financial terms, was Chairman of the Trustees until 1993, then President until his death in 1996.

1959 – 66 William HIggs lived at Little St Michael's as Resident Trustee, along with his wife, assisted by Custodian Mrs Christine Sanderson until 1963.

1966 – 79 John and Ida Simmons were employed by the Trust as Custodians, and lived in the house until John's death.

1973 – 4 The old Tor School buildings were demolished having been purchased by the Trust in the late 1960s, allowing the gardens to be developed below Arthur's Court to Chilkwell Street.

1979 Moya and Taras Kosikowski were appointed Custodians, living on site, presently joined by their son Sean, who was born in Vine Cottage in 1981.

1986 Leonard and Willa Sleath came from the Findhorn Foundation to take on the Wardenship of Chalice Well until past retiring age.

1996 Fred and Colleen Rosado from the USA took on the care of Chalice Well, adopting the title of 'Resident Guardians'.

1997 A new entrance was built on the site of the much older entrance.

1998 Michael and Lynne Orchard became resident Guardians until their resignation in 2005

1999 The Meeting Room was built with aid from a bequest made by late Trustee John Rowntree.

1993 – 2001 Roy Procter chaired the Trustees, Alan Gloak from 2001– 4. In 2005 Roy took over again temporarily, with co-chairperson Tyna Redpath, while new arrangements are being made for the ongoing care of the Well. The day to day business of Chalice Well is now being run by a group of dedicated staff rather than by a single or couple Guardian.

Chalice Well

entrance to garden
&
meeting room

Practicalities

How to find us:

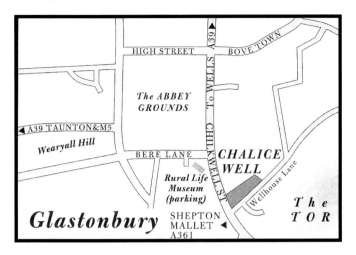

Chalice Well Gardens are open every day of the year, 10 am to 6 pm from April to October and for shorter hours in the winter. Check on www.chalicewell.org or phone 01458 831154.

The car park is very small and so availabale to visitors displaying disabled parking disks only. You may park at the Rural Life Museum with access via a pathway to Chilkwell Street.

For a modest annual subscription you could help maintain the material and spiritual health of this enchanting place by becoming a "Companion". Benefits of this family membership include free admission to the gardens, discounts in the shop, a regular newsletter, and the option to book into Little St Michael's Retreat House or Chalice Well Lodge. There will also be an invitation to "Companions' Day", an annual early summer event.

Alternatively you could become an "Active Supporter", with all the benefits of Companionship, by pledging a regular donation of time or money. Please enquire.

The shop is open for the same hours as the gardens. You may also visit it on line: www.chalicewellshop.com for mail order with secure payment facilities.

Bibliography

Alcock, Leslie, 1968, 'Excavations at South Cadbury Castle, 1967,' *Antiquities Journal*, Vol. XLVIII.

Ashe, Geoffrey, (1) 1968 (editor), *The Quest for Arthur's Britain*, London: Pall Mall. (2) 1979, *The Glastonbury Tor Maze*, Gothic Image. (3) 1982, *Avalonian Quest*, Methuen, London. (4) 1985, *The Rediscovery of King Arthur*, Henry Holt.

Benham, Patrick 1993, *The Avalonians*, Glastonbury, Gothic Image.

Bligh Bond, Frederick, (1) 1909, *The Architectural Handbook of Glastonbury Abbey*, Glastonbury. (2) 1918, *The Gate of Remembrance*, Oxford.

Bullied, Arthur, 1958, *The Lake Villages of Somerset*, (5th edition), Glastonbury.

Caine, Mary, 1978, *The Glastonbury Zodiac*, Kingston.

Bradley, Marion Zimmer, 1982, *The Mists of Avalon*.

Caradoc of Llancarfan, 'Vita Gildae' in *Gildas: The Ruin of Britain*, ed. Williams, Hugh, Cymmrodorion Record Series, No.3, Pt.2, London, 1901.

Carley, James P., (1) 1981, 'Melkin the Bard and Esoteric Tradition at Glastonbury Abbey', in *The Downside Review*, 99. (2) 1988, *Glastonbury Abbey*, Woodbridge: Boydell.

Coles, J. & Orme, B., (1) 1982, *Prehistory of the Somerset Levels*. Somerset Levels Project. (2) 1986, *Sweet Track to Glastonbury: The Somerset Levels in Prehistory*, London.

Cutting, Tracy, 2004, *Beneath the Silent Tor: The Life and Work of Alice Buckton*, Appleseed Press, Glastonbury.

Fortune, Dion 1934, *Avalon of the Heart*, (Aquarian Press 1971).

Geoffrey of Monmouth, *The History of the Kings of Britain*, Trans., Thorpe, L., Penguin, 1966.

Gildas: 'Life of Gildas' and 'Life of St Collen' in Baring-Gould, S. & Fisher, J., *Lives of the British Saints*, 1911.

Giraldus Cambrensis, *The Historical Works,* trans., Wright, T., Bohn, G., 1863.

Glasson, P. & Mann, N. 2005, *Avalon's Red & White Springs*, Green Magic, London.

Howard-Gordon, Frances, 1982, *Glastonbury: Maker of Myths*, Gothic Image.

Jones, Kathy, 1990, *The Goddess in Glastonbury*, Glastonbury.

John of Glastonbury, *Chronicle*, trans., Carley, B., Boydell 1985.

Lehmann, Rosamund, 1979, *My Dear Alexias*, Neville Spearman.

Lehmann, Rosamund and Tudor Pole, Wellesley, 1965 *A Man Seen Afar*, Neville Spearman.

Lewis, Lionel Smithett, 1922, *St. Joseph of Arimathea at Glastonbury*, Lutterworth Press, Cambridge.

Macintyre, Lorn, 1994, *Sir David Russell, A Biography*.

Maltwood, Katherine, 1929, *A Guide to Glastonbury's Temple of the Stars,* London.

Mann, Nicholas, (1) 1985, *The Cauldron and the Grail*, Glastonbury. (2) 1986, *Glastonbury Tor*, Glastonbury. (3) 2001, *The Isle of Avalon*, Green Magic, London. (4) 2004, *Secrets of Glastonbury Tor,* Green Magic, London.

Matthews, Benjamin, 1751, *The Virtues and Efficacy of the Water of Glastonbury*, London, (Somerset Studies Library, Taunton).

Michell, John,1990, *New Light on the Ancient Mysteries of Glastonbury*, Gothic Image, Glastonbury.

Miller, H. & Broadhurst, P. 1989, *The Sun and the Serpent*, Pendragon Press.

Nichols, Ross, 1975, *The Book of Druidry*, (1990).

Rahtz, Philip, (1) 1964, *Excavations at Chalice Well, Glastonbury*, P.S.A.N.H.S. Vol. 108, pp145-163. (2) 1971, *Excavations on Glastonbury Tor, Somerset, 1964-6*, R.A.I. (3)1993, *Glastonbury*, London.

Rahtz, P. & Hirst, S. 1974, *Beckery Chapel, Glastonbury, 1967-68*, Glastonbury.

Richardson, L., 1928, *Wells and Springs of Somerset*, Geological Survey, London.

Roberts, Anthony, 1978, *Glastonbury: Ancient Avalon, New Jerusalem*, Rider.

Sandys, Cynthia, 1986, *The Awakening Letters*, (2 volumes) C.W. Daniel, Saffron Walden.

Schwenk, Theodor, (1) 1965, *Sensitive Chaos: The Creation of Flowing Forms in Water and Air*, Steiner Press, London. (2) 1989, *Water: The Element of Life*, Anthropomorphic Press, Hudson NY.

Tudor Pole, Wellesley, (1) 1960, *The Silent Road*, Neville Spearman. (2) 1966, *Private Dowding*, Thetford Press. (3) 1968, *Writing on the Ground*, Neville Spearman.

Villiers, Oliver G, 1977, *Wellesley Tudor Pole. Appreciation & Valuation.*

William of Malmesbury, 'De Antiquitate Glastoniensis Ecclesiae', in Scott, J., *The Early History of Glastonbury*, Boydell, Woodbridge, 1981.

Wright, George W., (1) 1870, *The Chalice Well, or Blood Spring, and its Traditions*, Glastonbury Antiquarian Society Publication 1. (2) 1894, 'The History of Glastonbury During the Last Forty Years' in *Bulleids of Glastonbury*, Armynell Goodall, Taunton, 1984.